AS

AS

BLACK
RESISTANCE

FINDING
THE
CONDITIONS
FOR
LIBERATION

ZOÉ
SAMUDZI
AND
WILLIAM C.
ANDERSON

AS

RESIST

BLACK AS

ANCE

AK PRESS

© 2018 Zoé Samudzi
and William C. Anderson
ISBN: 978-1-84935-316-8
E-ISBN: 978-1-84935-315-1
LCCN: 2017957075

AK Press
370 Ryan Ave. #100
Chico, CA 95973
www.akpress.org
akpress@akpress.org

AK Press
33 Tower St.
Edinburgh EH6 7BN
Scotland
www.akuk.com
ak@akedin.demon.co.uk

The above addresses would
be delighted to provide you
with the latest AK Press
distribution catalog, which
features books, pamphlets,
zines, and stylish apparel
published and/or distributed
by AK Press. Alternatively,
visit our websites for the
complete catalog, latest
news, and secure ordering.

All image rights are retained
by the photographers, as noted
Cover and interior design
by Quemadura
Printed in Michigan
on acid-free paper

CONTENTS

FOREWORD

As Black as Resistance is a searing indictment of the U.S. settler colonial project and a call to action to save ourselves from the forces of oppression and tyranny. The philosophy of the book might well be summarized as "we're all we've got." This book appears in a chaotic time when the gap between rich and poor continues to grow, when climate change is causing mass devastation, when fascism appears resurgent, and when the ever-expanding carceral state is criminalizing and prematurely killing millions. In this context, William C. Anderson and Zoé Samudzi insist that our current political moment demands that we reject liberalism and embrace a more radical program to transform our conditions. They argue persuasively that grounding ourselves in the Black radical tradition offers the best path forward toward freedom and liberation.

In 1970, artist and activist Ossie Davis penned a preface for a reprint of the 1951 *We Charge Genocide* petition to the United Nations that contended with the historical debasement of Black people in the United States:

We say again, now: We will submit no further to the brutal in-dignities being practiced against us; we will not be intimidated, and most certainly not eliminated. We claim the ancient right of all peoples, not only to survive unhindered, but also to par-ticipate as equals in man's inheritance here on earth. We fight to preserve ourselves, to see that the treasured ways of our life-in-common are not destroyed by brutal men or heedless institutions.[1]

Davis stresses, like Anderson and Samudzi do, that Black people have been consistently subjected to inordinate violence, considered disposable and easily killable. In the late nineteenth century, a remark was attributed to a southern police chief who suggested that there were three types of homicides: "If a nigger kills a white man, that's murder. If a white man kills a nigger, that's justifiable homicide. If a nigger kills a nigger, that's one less nigger."[2] White supremacy has always held Black life cheap. Davis's words embody defiance and so do those written by Anderson and Samudzi. Just as Davis claims an inherent right to

1. William L Patterson, *We Charge Genocide: The Crime of Government against the Negro People* (New York City: International Publishers, 1970), v.

2. Manfred Berg, *Popular Justice: A History of Lynching in America* (Lanham: Rowman & Littlefield, 2011), 116.

self-defense, *As Black as Resistance* highlights a long tradition in Black communities by people like Robert F. Williams, who invoked the right to armed self-defense.

In 1955, Williams joined the NAACP in his hometown of Monroe, North Carolina, after having served in the U.S. Marine Corps. He quickly became president of the chapter and rebuilt it to include many veterans, farmers, and working-class people. In 1956, the Monroe NAACP started a campaign to integrate the only swimming pool in the city. It had been built with federal funds, yet blacks were barred from access. City officials not only refused to let blacks swim in the pool, they also turned down requests to build a pool that they could use. Williams and the Monroe NAACP took the city to court. This engendered massive backlash from the local white community, including members of the Ku Klux Klan. The KKK held rallies, drove around Black neighborhoods intimidating residents, and fired guns at people out of moving cars.

When ministers asked local politicians to intervene to prevent the KKK from driving through Black neighborhoods and terrorizing residents, they were told that the Klan had "as much constitutional right to organize as the NAACP." Williams and the NAACP petitioned the governor and even President Eisenhower for support and assistance. They received no help.

Williams and other members of the NAACP decided then that it was time to take matters into their own hands. If the government would not protect their communities, then they would arm themselves. The Monroe NAACP applied for and received a charter from the National Rifle Association. By the end of one year, their NRA club had over sixty members.

During the summer of 1957, an armed motorcade of Klan members got into a firefight with Williams and other NAACP members. The Klan had opened fire on the home of the Monroe NAACP vice president, Dr. Albert E. Perry. Williams and his colleagues successfully turned the Klan motorcade back. The incident would make national news and begin to bring more attention to Williams. In his book *Negroes with Guns*, he clearly lays out his rationale for advocating armed self-defense:

> The stranglehold of oppression cannot be loosened by a plea to the oppressor's conscience. Social change in something as fundamental as racist oppression involves violence. You cannot have progress here without violence and upheaval, because it's a struggle for survival for one and a struggle for liberation for the other. Always the powers in command are ruthless and unmerciful in defending their position and their privileges. This is not an abstract rule to be meditated upon by Americans. This

is a truth that was revealed at the birth of America, and has continued to be revealed many times in our history. The principle of self-defense is an American tradition that began at Lexington and Concord.[3]

Williams was an inspiration to Huey P. Newton who cofounded the Black Panther Party for Self-Defense in 1966 about a decade after Williams had assumed control over the Monroe NAACP. The Black Panther Party is invoked in *As Black as Resistance*, and we have a lot to learn from it. While liberals celebrate nonviolent resistance, we can't forget that many Black radicals have advocated the use of violence in response to being attacked. As we struggle against a renewed fascism today, we continue to wrestle with these issues raised in the book.

As an abolitionist, the Black anarchism espoused by Anderson and Samudzi resonates with me. Abolishing the prison industrial complex (PIC) is not just about ending prisons but also about creating an alternative system of governance that is not based on domination, hierarchy, and control. In that respect, abolitionism and anarchism are positive rather than negative projects. They do not signal

3. Robert F. Williams, *Negroes with Guns* (Detroit: Wayne State University Press, 1998), 72.

the absence of prisons or governments but the creation of different forms of sociality, governance, and accountability that are not statist and carceral.

In this respect, this work echoes the practices of anarcha-indigenism that differentiate inclusive models of indigenous nationhood based on inclusivity, horizontality, and interrelatedness from nation-states based on borders, exclusivity, domination, and control. Thus, the politics of abolition require us to see, as Angela Davis notes in *Are Prisons Obsolete?*, that prisons cannot be abolished without a complete restructuring of society. Abolitionism is sometimes disassociated from the larger political vision from which it emerges. However, the politics expressed in *As Black as Resistance* invite us not to simply critique prisons or the state but to imagine and then build alternative forms of governance that are life-giving. It is a book brimming with urgency and one that boldly confronts the injustices of our past and present. It is a book that reminds us of our power to collectively make transformative changes that will improve the lives of the many over the few. It is a book of revolutionary hope that pierces the despair and fear of our current political moment.

ACKNOWLEDGMENTS

Any attempt at a complete list of names to acknowledge would surely result in failure, so I won't even attempt that which I know will end incomplete. Instead I would like to mention why I'm thankful for the people closest to me. There are some who truly know who I am, and it isn't necessarily measured by time, proximity, or even blood. It's measured by sincerity and understanding.

Conversations brought this work together and drive much of my writing. Those of you who have cared enough to listen to my ideas and my rants over the phone and through texts are in my writing and close to my heart. You've heard me cleaning; you've heard me cooking; you've heard me running errands; but most importantly, you've heard me while I toil over how to convey what I feel needs to be written. You know I try to write what needs to be written, and this book by Zoé and me is definitely a huge part of that.

As of late I've truly begun to see just how much family influences who we are as people, specifically the ancestors we never knew. So I would like to thank the activists, writers, and fighters who came before me on both sides of my family. I know I would not be who I am nor would I be here at all if it weren't for you. I'm so grateful to my loving parents (especially my late mother, Janice, who was as close to perfection as a mother could be) for encouraging and influencing me. I'm appreciative of my dear sister Ashley, her husband Anthony, and their family for their love and support. I appreciate all of my nieces and my nephew who I know love me and who I love so dearly.

My friend and co-author Zoé, I appreciate you so much for agreeing to this journey and I have love for who you are. Your mind and your contributions to this book are great things the world needs to know about. Let's keep working towards the liberation we know people deserve.

Generally, thank you to everyone who has read my writing and who has pushed me and urged me to continue when I wasn't always sure of myself. Thank you to the great editors and writers I read who have helped me feel inspired. And, my goodness, a grand thank you to the other artists: the musicians, poets, painters, dancers, and so on who keep me alive through their work. Thank you to the organizers and teachers who showed me what it means to care. I would also like to thank my enemies and adversaries as well. I appreciate y'all for teaching me so much about myself and what I hope to be in this life.

Today feels clear to me. So many things that were supposed to happen and should happen in the future have come to me like a subtle wind nudging me forward. I'm thankful.

WILLIAM C. ANDERSON

First and foremost, my deepest gratitude is owed to Black women. Each and every day, I am nurtured intellectually and made whole emotionally by the labor and care that the Black women pour into the world; I feel indebted to that labor because I am sustained by that labor. While individual scholars and thinkers may not be explicitly cited, their frameworks and analyses and insights comprise the core of my own work. Just as it is vital for me to acknowledge the Black feminist canon, I must also acknowledge the critical and generative work of Black leftists, particularly Black anarchists. Regardless of sectarian difference, I am indebted to the countless conversations I've had and all measures of generous support I've received and inspiration I've gleaned from so many friends and comrades whose urgent liberatory missions I share. And thank you endlessly to the scores of friends who've taught me and fed me and shared with me and held me and soothed me and encouraged me; thank you to my dearest friend, Antoinette Myers, in particular, for never letting me quit.

I can't begin to articulate my gratitude to all my family. Thank you to my mum and dad for instilling within me an intense curiosity and a thirst to wonder and learn and write and read and do more. Thank you to my brother and sister-in-law for always giving me a safe supportive space to work or escape from my work. Thank you to my new nephew, Ariko, who's made me the happiest *tete* in the world: for teaching me so much about what it means to love unconditionally and how to channel a fierce love into my work and everything else I do. Thank you to my *sekuru*, a freedom fighter, who still teaches me what it means to think and speak like and be a revolutionary. My deepest gratitude, as always and in everything I do, is owed to my ancestors whose knowledge I am grateful for and whose anticolonial resistance I hope to embody in all I do.

I am grateful to Jerome Roos for giving us the space in *ROAR Magazine* that eventually led to this book. Thank you also to the team at AK Press for making this entire process so manageable; thank you Andrew for coaxing out the words and ideas that existed just under the surface but weren't always readily available.

Thank you, of course, to William. Thank you for extending to me an almost otherworldly patience, thank you for trusting me to co-author your first book. Thank you always for the intense care and thoughtfulness you put into your work, and the care you have for those around you and have always extended to me without hesitation. I so deeply appreciate you.

Thank you to everyone I'll never meet or who I've not yet met, but who share in a vision of Black liberation. This book is for me and the people I love, and this book is for you too. This book is for everyone.

Pamberi ne hondo! Pamberi ne chimurenga!

ZOÉ SAMUDZI

AS

AS RESI

BLACK

STANCE

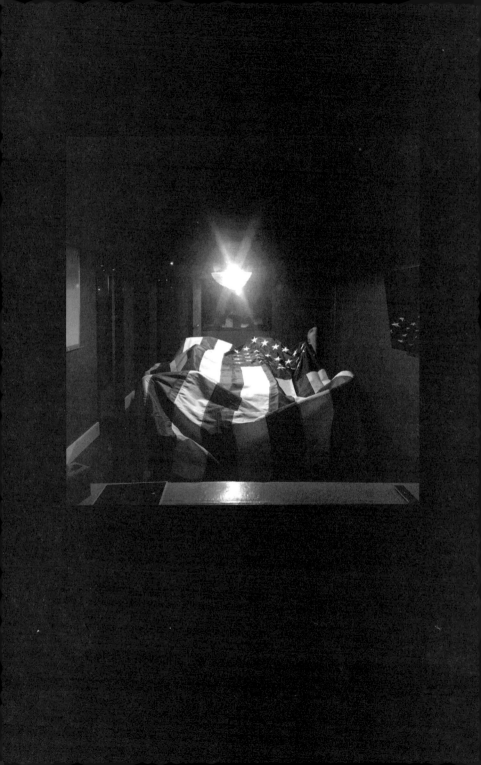

CHAPTER ONE

BLACK IN ANARCHY

The United States has experienced cycles of tyranny since its inception. For some, the United States represents *only* this experience. A disillusioned liberal establishment has begun to worry that this country might be losing its democracy. However, the democracy some fear to lose was never achieved for many of us in the first place. The ability to participate in U.S. society has been an ongoing struggle for the descendants of the colonized, enslaved, immigrants, and asylum seekers. The U.S. empire has caused trauma endlessly from the first moment it existed. Frederick Douglass asserted:

> What, to the American slave, is your 4th of July? I answer; a day that reveals to him, more than all other days in the year, the gross injustice and cruelty to which he is the constant victim. To him, your celebration is a sham; your boasted liberty, an unholy license; your national greatness, swelling vanity; your

sounds of rejoicing are empty and heartless; your denunciation of tyrants brass fronted impudence; your shout of liberty and equality, hollow mockery; your prayers and hymns, your sermons and thanksgivings, with all your religious parade and solemnity, are to him, mere bombast, fraud, deception, impiety, and hypocrisy—a thin veil to cover up crimes which would disgrace a nation of savages. There is not a nation on the earth guilty of practices more shocking and bloody than are the people of the United States, at this very hour.[1]

We must we expand the scope of Douglass's question beyond celebrations of national independence. We who rightly take issue with the national project must also ask: Is the American Revolution the singular, purposefully romanticized tale of wealthy landowners refusing taxation and splitting from the British crown? Or is there another potential American revolution that has yet to occur?

It is deeply ironic that we are taught the glories of the U.S. birth through revolutionary resistance to the British

1. From Frederick Douglass speech, Rochester, New York, July 5, 1852, at an event commemorating the signing of the Declaration of Independence. Douglass, "The Meaning of July Fourth for the Negro," History Is a Weapon, www.historyisaweapon.com/defcon1/douglassjuly4 .html.

empire but told today we must not resist, must not be revolutionary, and need to resolve differences through "reasoned dialogue" and civic engagement. Equating a revolt to escape unfair monarchical taxes to real revolution is a perversion of the concept of "revolution" itself. How revolutionary were men who saw no problems with enslavement and citizenship based on white manhood and land ownership? This "revolution" served white supremacist patriotism and the suppression of dissent. Revolt is at the foundation of the United States, yet now patience and cooperation are presented as the only acceptable ways to address inequity. The very ideals at the foundation of the state are denounced while the state itself monopolizes the right to "legitimate" revolutionary change (just as it monopolizes the right to "legitimate" uses of force and self-defense). After all, the second paragraph of the Declaration of Independence reads:

> We hold these truths to be self-evident, that all men are created equal, that they are endowed by their Creator with certain unalienable Rights, that among these are Life, Liberty and the pursuit of Happiness.—That to secure these rights, Governments are instituted among Men, deriving their just powers from the consent of the governed, that *whenever any Form of Govern-*

ment becomes destructive of these ends, it is the Right of the People to alter or to abolish it, and to institute new Government, laying its foundation on such principles and organizing its powers in such form, as to them shall seem most likely to effect their Safety and Happiness" [our emphasis].

Black people entered this settler colony through transatlantic kidnapping, chattel trade (being bought and sold as property), and forced servitude. Indigenous genocide and land expropriation (and enclosure) are intrinsic to American settlement.[2] And the use of Black labor was responsible for settler agricultural expansion and the growth of the southern agrarian economy. Once successfully cleared and claimed by white settlers, "[Native] land would be mixed with Black labor to produce cotton, the white gold of the

---

2. "Enclosure" here refers to the process of privatizing and territorializing for settler use Indigenous land that had been held and used as public commons. Enclosure requires the clearance of land, and this occurred through forced removal of Native peoples by the U.S. government. One famous example is the 1830 Indian Removal Act, signed by Andrew Jackson, which led to the forced relocation of Cherokee, Muscogee, Choctaw, Creek, and Seminole people, commonly known as the "Trail of Tears," from the southeastern United States. This process is the entry point for a Marxian analysis of primitive accumulation, which enables broader capitalistic hoarding of resources and capital, private ownership, and inequity.

Deep South."[3] It is through the institution of slavery that Black people entered the American social contract. Slavery—forced servitude—was imposed upon Black people throughout the United States, and blackness thus became a marker of that enslavement that would continue even after slavery's demise. Race in the United States evolved not only as a social identity, but also as a property relation, which was codified in the American legal system and within the social contract itself.[4] Inherent to liberal social contract values is the simultaneous maintenance of white supremacy's capital interests, signified by anti-Indigenous and anti-Black exclusions,[5] and the purported values of equality: liberalism pays lip service to egalitarianism while

3. Patrick Wolfe, "Settler Colonialism and the Elimination of the Native," *Journal of Genocide Research* 8, no. 4 (2006): 387–409.

4. Cheryl L. Harris. "Whiteness as Property," *Harvard Law Review* 106, no. 8 (1993): 1707–1791.

5. Charles Mills's *The Racial Contract* (Ithaca: Cornell University Press, 1997) characterizes this social contract as "not a contract between everybody ('we the people'), but between people who count, the people who really are people ('we the white people')," 3. Racism is not an aberration of a foundationally equal social contract, but the result of the stratification built into it: "From the inception, then, race is in no way an 'afterthought,' a 'deviation,' from ostensibly raceless Western ideals, but rather a central shaping constituent of those ideals," 14.

complementing and structurally lending itself to fascistic logics and political encroachments.[6] "Societal fascism" describes the process and political logics of state formation wherein entire populations are excluded or ejected from the social contract. They are pre-contractually excluded because they have never been a part of a given social contract and never will be, or they are ejected from a contract they were previously a part of and are only able to enjoy conditional inclusion at best. This differs from the political fascism represented, for example, by the regimes of Benito Mussolini, Francisco Franco, Adolf Hitler, and others. It nevertheless lends itself to the formation of a political system easily susceptible to authoritarianism because it is grounded in inequity and inequality, and marked by political mechanisms and a popular consensus that allow rights and liberties to legally be taken away in the event that individuals and communities are ejected from the social contract.[7]

Black Americans are residents of a settler colony, not truly citizens of the United States. Despite a constitution

6. Alexander Reid Ross's *Against the Fascist Creep* (Chico, CA: AK Press, 2017) provides a useful analysis of ideologies and conditions that enable the "fascist creep."

7. Boaventura de Sousa Santos, "Nuestra America: Reinventing a Subaltern Paradigm of Recognition and Redistribution." *Theory, Culture & Society* 18, nos. 2–3 (2001): 185–217.

laden with European Enlightenment values and a document of independence declaring certain inalienable rights, Black existence was legally that of private property until postbellum emancipation. The Black American condition today is an evolved condition directly connected to this history of slavery,[8] and that will continue to be the case as long as the United States remains as an ongoing settler project. Nothing short of a complete dismantling of the American state as it presently exists can or will disrupt this.

As Hortense Spillers makes explicit in her influential work, "Mama's Baby, Papa's Maybe: An American Grammar Story," blackness was indelibly marked and transformed through the transatlantic slave trade. European colonialism and the process of African enslavement—both as a profit-maximizing economic institution and a dehumanizing institution—can be regarded as "high crimes against the *flesh*, as the person of African females and males registered the wounding."[9] Crimes against the flesh are not sim-

8. See Saidiya Hartman's *Lose Your Mother: A Journey along the Atlantic Slave Route* (New York: Farrar, Strauss, and Giroux, 2007) for a Black feminist genealogy and transatlantic analysis of the afterlife of slavery.

9. Hortense Spillers, "Mama's Baby, Papa's Maybe: An American Grammar Story," *Diacritics* 17, no. 2 (1987): 64–81.

ply crimes against the corporeal self: the wounded flesh, rather, was the personhood and social position of the African. The wounding is the process of blackening through subjugation, a wound from which Black people and blackness writ large have yet to recover. Recovery, a positive reassertion of identity, is impossible. We are Black because we are oppressed by the state; we are oppressed by the state because we are Black.[10] Black existence within the social contract is existence within a heavily regulated state, a state in which our emancipation from enslavement was not a singular event or a moment of true actualization of freedom but rather a state-sanctioned transition from forced servitude to anti-Black subjection and exclusion.[11] We are carriers of the coveted blue passport still trapped in a zone of [citizen] nonbeing, a zone where we are not fully disap-

10. This is an adaption of the tautology within colonial logic as articulated in Frank Wilderson III's "Gramsci's Black Marx: Whither the Slave in Civil Society" (*Social Identities* 2003) (and previously by Frantz Fanon in *Wretched of the Earth*): "The most ridiculous question a black person can ask a cop is, 'why did you shoot me?' How does one account for the gratuitous? The cop is at a disadvantage: 'I shot you because you are black; you are black because I shot you.'"

11. Saidiya V. Hartman, *Scenes of Subjection: Terror, Slavery, and Self-Making in Nineteenth-Century America* (New York: Oxford University Press, 1997).

peared and eliminated but where we are still denied the opportunity and ability to self-determine: a state of precarity
that only allows for the conditional survival of particular
bodies in particular ways.[12] Frantz Fanon writes:

> The zone where the natives live is not complementary to the
> zone inhabited by the settlers. *The two zones are opposed, but
> not in the service of a higher unity.* Obedient to the rules of
> pure Aristotelian logic, they both follow the principle of recip-
> rocal exclusivity. No conciliation is possible, for of the two
> terms, one is superfluous. The settlers' town is a strongly built
> town, all made of stone and steel. It is a brightly lit town; the
> streets are covered with asphalt, and the garbage cans swal-
> low all the leavings, unseen, unknown and hardly thought
> about. The settler's feet are never visible, except perhaps in the
> sea; but there you're never close enough to see them. His feet
> are protected by strong shoes although the streets of his town
> are clean and even, with no holes or stones. The settler's town
> is a well-fed town, an easygoing town; its belly is always full
> of good things. The settler's town is a town of white people, of
> foreigners. The town belonging to the colonized people, or at

12. Isabell Lorey, *State of Insecurity: Government of the Precarious*
(London: Verso Books, 2015).

least the native town, the Negro village, the medina, the reservation, is a place of ill fame, peopled by men of evil repute. They are born there, it matters little where or how; they die there, it matters not where, nor how. It is a world without spaciousness; men live there on top of each other, and their huts are built one on top of the other. The native town is a hungry town, starved of bread, of meat, of shoes, of coal, of light. The native town is a crouching village, a town on its knees, a town wallowing in the mire. It is a town of niggers and dirty Arabs. . . . *This world divided into compartments, this world cut in two is inhabited by two different species.* [our emphases][13]

Within this zone, blackness is constantly under surveillance. This is not simply an allusion to the state's literal surveillance projects (like COINTELPRO, the covert FBI program that destroyed so many mid-twentieth-century Black radical efforts).[14] We refer rather to settler colonial

13. Frantz Fanon, "On Violence," Chapter 1 in *Wretched of the Earth*, (New York City: Grove Press, 1963).

14. The FBI's Counterintelligence Program, COINTELPRO, began in 1956 with a mission to target, infiltrate, and destroy individuals and groups deemed subversive by the government. This included anti–Vietnam War organizers; communist and socialist groups; ethnic and race-based liberation groups like the Black Panthers, the Young Lords, and

arrangements in anti-blackness and anti-indigeneity that co-create the framework for state racial formations.[15] The mechanisms comprising anti-Black surveillance were foundational to post-9/11 "War on Terror" securitization of Muslim, immigrant, and refugee communities across the United States. These suspensions of rights and civil liberties in favor of order are not new. They are rather being explicitly applied to another racialized group both domestically and in U.S. foreign policy. Where Islamism constitutes the enemy abroad, blackness is the perpetual enemy at home. Islamophobic and anti-Black logics become complementary (and also inextricably linked where the first Muslims in the United States were enslaved West Africans). What is citizenship within a social contract where our Sixth Amendment right to a fair trial can be suspended in the event of our completely legal (but extrajudicial) murder by police?

the American Indian Movement; and individuals linked to the civil rights movement, including Martin Luther King Jr., Malcolm X, and Fred Hampton, who was murdered during a COINTELPRO joint operation with the Chicago Police Department in 1969.

15. Simone Browne's *Dark Matter: On the Surveillance of Blackness* (Durham: Duke University Press, 2015) is a striking interrogation of this process-phenomenon.

Black liberation poses an existential threat to white supremacy because the existence of free Black people necessitates a complete transformation and destruction of this settler state. The United States cannot exist without Black subjection, and, in this way, articulated racial formations revolve in large part around anti-Black regulations. It is impossible to reform the system of racial capitalism. Those who believe in and operate according to the laws of white supremacy are not solely white people, though beneficiaries are largely and most visibly white. The supporters of this system include an internally oppressed multiracial coalition.

There are many politicians and state operatives of color, Black and otherwise, working for white supremacy. Diversity in the seats of power will not solve our problems. Simply because someone shares race, gender, or another aspect of identity does not guarantee loyalty or that they will act in the best interests of Black communities. We adopt a self-sacrificial politic in expressing openness or friendliness to the state because some of its functionaries look like us. U.S. political systems were not designed to meet our needs, and sweetening our concerns with rhetorics of "diversity" and "inclusion" will merely enable nominal representation (or a mitigation of material harms in some cases) as opposed to liberation in any real sense.

Because white supremacists helming the state understand the liberatory potential of Black radicalism, these energies have been co-opted into safer and more respectable means of effecting change. Black America has become effectively trapped in the never-ending cycle of partisan politics: between the actively antagonistic Grand Old Party and the Democratic Party that exploits Black loyalty but offers few paths for any substantial improvement of the Black condition. The U.S. political cycle and the inner workings of the election process clearly leave much to be desired. The people inside this hopeless maze of civic duty often feel so uninspired that they remove themselves from the process, choosing not to vote or otherwise engage in elections. This decision is not a failure of the people who choose not to participate but a failure of the system itself.

Whether most citizens can explain why the Electoral College system has been a failure (or why it works) is of no consequence. Low voter turnout shows that participation feels like an empty gesture, and it is just that to a large extent, especially when political outcomes are manipulated by mass voter disenfranchisement, redistricting, and a system of indirect representation and democracy. The Electoral College system is not a reliable vehicle for change, certainly not for much needed social transformation. At the 1787 Constitutional Convention, a popular vote count for president would have made states that predominantly relied on slavery much less likely to win national elections. The Electoral College, which was based on population, was seen as leveling the playing field. Subsequently each state's decision to cast electoral votes has been in the hands of the electors, who are not bound to vote the way the public did in the states they represent. The convention decided to count each enslaved person as three-fifths of a human, and this dehumanizing convenience became known as the "Three-fifths Compromise."

This history of the Electoral College inheres in what takes place during national elections today. A candidate can be elected president of the United States despite another candidate receiving more votes overall. This was the case with George W. Bush's election in 2000 and then Donald Trump's victory over Hillary Clinton in 2016. States with more electors have unequal power in a national election, which often feels far more like a calculated game than a democratic process serving to meet constituents' needs. Furthermore, electors—those who selected to make up the Electoral College—are not bound by law to vote for the candidate a state's voters have chosen. Our votes are symbolic, and the process doesn't necessarily result in victory for the people's choice. It doesn't even guarantee the commitment of the electors.

Under the current system, in which the Democratic and Republican Party are each invested, political discourse is constantly being pulled to the right. Liberals position themselves as the "lesser of two evils" against the Republicans in every election, banking on their electability as the arguably better choice while consistently failing to offer protective and supportive policies to counter Republican ones. This clearly demonstrates that the liberal establishment knows that this system is disempowering. It continues to encourage people to happily and willingly engage in the system while it effectively self-sabotages at each opportunity.

When we allow the Democratic Party leaders to position the party as the moral authority against a worse party, we risk condoning all of what the "less evil" candidate represents. We participate in and perpetuate this cycle of disempowerment. The Democratic Party has grown increasingly conservative over the years due to this policy of compromise and lesser evilism. The party shifts to the right because it doesn't seek to portray itself as real opposition but only an easy and un-alienating alternative. The liberal class and establishment party politics here are partially responsible for the continued shift to the right, not only in this country but also globally. U.S. politics are exported throughout the West and influence the climates of other countries that are susceptible to U.S. foreign policy's powerful influence. This is one of the many reasons a true Left and a real opposition in this country is absolutely necessary. Otherwise, the Right will continue to grow in its systemic influence, and authoritarianism will naturally grow stronger, both within the government and outside of it. Because there is not a unified Left in this country, the work of the scattered leftists is imperative. If we do not build that functionally cohesive Left (or at least pragmatically recognize the necessity for inter-sectarian work), the rights of all people oppressed by capitalist white supremacy will inevitably continue to erode.

Some might hope that tyrannical political trends that come with the aforementioned shift to the right can be useful to the Left as a mobilizing and organizing impetus. One might think that in a country with as much comfort as the United States, the mild to severe discomfort brought on by increasingly authoritarian discourses and policy might inspire people to fight harder. But attempting to coax people from their relative comfort zones and into the streets is difficult. U.S. empire was an affront to humanity long before this political moment, and the problems we face today have existed for generations. Though we are admittedly not yet able to fully articulate or agree upon what it may look like, we ultimately work toward total and complete freedom—we do not just the hope for it, we strive to realize it in any way that we can—and this cannot come from idealistic (and ultimately empty) representations of political heroes and saviors. Our ideas of what freedom and liberation mean to us must rest on something sturdier than the shoulders of charismatic and seemingly progressive politicians. We must define those for ourselves. We should not wait for the magic words we want to hear come out of someone else's mouth when we can designate, dictate, and deliver change ourselves. We should not sit back and wait for politicians to grant us our humanity, a humanity that has always existed and it should not be left to elections, political terms, or waiting periods to determine whether or not we will see it actualized.

Legendary singer Nina Simone once described freedom as "no fear," a description that undoubtedly resonates with many. What does fear have to do with freedom? We know that when we and our communities and families are not guaranteed our humanity and the circumstances we need to flourish, we are often afraid, even terrified. To be *without* that fear could truly be gratifying, even liberatory. Fear pervades so many aspects of our everyday lives as Black people: the fear of eviction, of police, of airport security, immigration enforcement, and illnesses we simply cannot afford to suffer. Uncertainty and the fear of being unsafe and not having the resources necessary to survive can consume us, leaving no time to work for the world we truly want to see: we become more consumed in work to stabilize ourselves and our communities rather than spending more time and resources on generative and rehabilitating work.

A question arises from all of this: which fear is greater, the fear of the pain we know or the pain we do not? Surely many would choose the latter as greater because a familiar pain seems more bearable. But our pain threshold is being pushed to its limits in a hamster wheel that seems to be spinning faster. We cannot even really claim the fear we know because this seems to be growing increasingly urgent. That leaves us with a suggestion brought on by circumstance: to overcome our fears, if we should choose, in pursuit of something better. This is obviously easier said than done. Defiance is scary, but we seem continuously headed in the wrong direction. What if we change course and embrace the unknown despite our fear? That would require a collective courage we have yet to draw upon en masse.

CHAPTER TWO

WHAT LANDS ON US

Through enslavement in the Americas and histories of indigeneity and migration on the African continent, Black identity is in many ways inextricably linked to land. Most African people can be understood as being indigenous to Africa to the extent that their origins are exclusively from the African continent. "Indigenous," however, is usually applied to members of groups and communities comprising nations within (and predating) larger nation-states, and lands of indigenous nations do not correspond to lands enclosed by international borders. Indigenous communities in Africa include the Twa people scattered across the African Great Lakes, Zambia, and western Uganda; the Maasai and Samburu peoples of Kenya and Tanzania; the Nuba people of Sudan; the Khoikhoi (or Khoi) and the San of southern and southeastern Africa; and the Dogon of Mali and Burkina Faso, and many others. As these different peoples experience marginalization from the state, many have sought to establish their sovereignty and protect their individual and collective rights through state mechanisms, transnational bodies (e.g., the African Union's African Commission on Human and Peoples' Rights and the Indigenous Peoples of Africa Co-ordinating Committee), and international means (e.g., the United Nations Declaration on the Rights of Indigenous Peoples and the UN Permanent Forum on Indigenous Peoples).

Prior to the disruption and erosion of African societal structures through colonial incorporation into global capitalism, many of the continent's societies revolved around land-based and pastoral communalism—they were collectively oriented and based on the idea of community ownership.[1] Through the forced extraction of Africans during the transatlantic slave trade, blackness has come to sym-

1. See Sam Mbah and I. E. Igariwey's *African Anarchism: The History of a Movement* (Tucson: See Sharp Press, 1997) for a useful description of African socio-economic transitions and integration into global capitalist systems. The word "communalism" is not used with any intent to idealize or homogenize the array of different precolonial social and political organizations on the continent. While these horizontal structures were common, hierarchies and inequities were also frequent within them (often along the lines of gender and sexual identities).

bolize a kind of rootlessness. This mass kidnapping and genocidal trafficking forced the reconstruction of enslaved peoples' ethnic and cultural identities outside of the lands from which they were stolen. To ensure a cohesive, unified anticolonial struggle and liberation, ethnic identities were de-prioritized in favor of newly rendered national identities. The establishment of a British settler colony in what is now Zimbabwe, for example, saw the consolidation of and drawing of colonial boundaries around Mashonaland and Matabeleland, which were declared British protectorates in 1891. One function of these borders unforeseen by colonizers was unifying national identity around which indigenous peoples within those boundaries could unite. In the words of nationalist leader Joshua Nkomo, following the delineation of boundaries previously disputed and defined "only by [indigenous] custom," there was "no reason why all of us should not unite and develop an unquestioned national identity." In 1977, soon-to-be Zimbabwean prime minister (and later president) Robert Mugabe articulated a similar sentiment, though from a different ethnic position than Nkomo, a Ndebele, naturalizing an essential Shona quality within an apparently historically existent Shona nation. Zimbabwean national identity, however, has never been unquestioned or uncontested, and class, gender, urban-rural divisions and competition, and ethnopolitics continue to fragment notions of "national unity" and shape the contours of national politics. Though formation differed depending on the state and the colonial processes within it and the constructed myth of national identity, a "pre-existing unified ideological or political subject that could quickly be mobilized against colonial rule" prevailed in Zimbabwe and in other African states.[2]

Much of the identity production of Black people in the United States, both from descendants of enslaved Africans (African Americans) and otherwise, has stemmed from a sense of yearning: an attempt to reconcile a diasporic self with roots and a sense of African groundedness, a sense of home space. Certain strains of Black nationalist thought and politics historically (and even presently) have called for Black people in America to go "back to Africa." This nationalism, driven by logics of land-based reparations for expropriated labor in the United States and abduction from the continent, voids the sovereignty of African states.

2. Brian Raftopoulos and A. S. Mlambo, eds., "Introduction: The Hard Road to Becoming National," in *Becoming Zimbabwe: A History from the Pre-Colonial Period to 2008* (Johannesburg: Jacana Media, 2009), xvii–xix.

Black nationalism in the United States can sometimes en-
tail these quasi-settler claims to land, whether through
Black Zionist traditions or land-based reparations claims
entailing the establishment of a Black nation within former Confederate states. Black Zionism evoked the Exodus
story of Moses leading the Israelites out of bondage from
Egypt and into the Promised Land, a clear analogy to the
Black diaspora's potential liberation from the subjugation
of American white supremacy. Marcus Garvey's "back to
Africa" politics, for example, emulated the Zionist concept
of *aliyah*, the return immigration of Jewish refugees in the
diaspora to Israel. While a tenet of Zionism, it was not established as large-scale until the late nineteenth century
and then, on an even greater scale, after Israel's creation
in 1948. By contrast, Palestinian refugees displaced by the
Nakba (1948) or Six-Day War (1967) are not afforded the
right of return granted to them under international law.[3]

3. "Nakba" refers to the mass exodus and expulsion of Palestinians
from their homes in 1948 following the creation of the state of Israel that
same year. In his book *Palestine ... It Is Something Colonial*, Hatem
Bazian describes the expulsion as "'*an original Zionist sin*' that planned
and saw to it the expulsion and dispossession of Palestine's indigenous in-
habitants and forced them into refugee camps and permanent Diaspora."
In *The Ethnic Cleansing of Palestine* (London: Oneworld Publications,
2006), Ilan Pappé describes the Nakba as a part of "the inevitable product

Founded in 1968, the secessionist Republic of New Afrika was an organization and social movement founded on the basis of three major goals. Leaders sought the creation of an independent Black nation in the southeastern states (the former Confederate States of America), a nation that would include Georgia, Alabama, South Carolina, Mississippi, and Louisiana; $7 billion in financial reparations to Black American descendants of enslaved people; and a nationwide referendum for all African-Americans to vote on whether or not they wished to remain U.S. citizens. More controversial than Black secessionism itself is the question of the fate of the Native American communities in those states. Where would their struggle for liberation and autonomous nationhood fit within the Republic of New Afrika framework? Would their sovereignty be erased and subsumed?

"Settler colonialism" refers to the process through which an external force colonizes a space through the

---

of the Zionist ideological impulse to have an exclusively Jewish presence in Palestine": it was an implementation of "the ideological vision of an ethnically cleansed Palestine" that left more than half of the country's native population (nearly 800,000 people) displaced. Needless to say, the fact that the word "nakba" means "disaster" or "catastrophe" is tragically apt.

establishment of permanent settlements "with the aim of permanently securing their hold on specific locales" through a claim of "special sovereign charge" or dominion over a space.[4] The kind of colonialism that marked the majority of the world was one that necessitated the existence of indigenous communities for a labor force, among other things. By contrast, settler colonialism is a far more invasive mode of colonialism that is marked by the "dispensability" of indigenous communities. It is a "project whose dominant feature is not exploitation but replacement," driven by a ruling logic of a "sustained institutional tendency to eliminate the Indigenous population."[5] Settler "invasion is a structure not an event," Patrick Wolfe critically notes. Examples of settler colonies include the United States, Canada, Australia, South Africa, Zimbabwe, and Israel. The creation of each of these states was predicated upon the displacement and *removal* of longstanding native communities that existed within the borders of the nation-

4. Lorenzo Veracini, *Settler Colonialism: A Theoretical Overview* (London: Palgrave Macmillan, 2010), 3.

5. Patrick Wolfe, *Settler Colonialism and the Transformation of Anthropology: The Politics and Poetics of an Ethnographic Event* (London: Cassell, 1999), 163.

states. Because Africans were forcibly removed from the continent and trafficked to the United States and did not largely participate in the European process of domination (with, of course, notable exception made for the so-called Buffalo Soldiers, African American army regiments that participated in the Indian Wars), Black people cannot be considered as settlers in the United States. Though we may participate in ongoing settler processes and ultimately benefit from the elimination of Indigenous people and the expropriation of their land, we are not settlers. But championing the creation of a Black majoritarian nation-state, where the fate of Indigenous people is ambiguous at best, is an idea rooted in settler logic. Is settler adjacency what a truly intersectional framework and multifaceted approach to Black liberation entails? If we use the creation of the state of Israel as an example, the ultimate reparation for historical violence is the opportunity to become a colonizer and gain proximity to (or entrance into) whiteness. Although popularly positioned as a kind of reparation for the mass murder of millions of Jewish people in the German Holocaust, the creation of Israel was as an act of European antisemitism in the eyes of some, including Israeli scholar Ilan Pappé. The establishment of a Jewish homeland meant that antagonistic Western governments—states such as the

United States and Allied Powers that were aware of the genocidal violence of Adolf Hitler's Final Solution[6] but stood idly by and even sought to appease the Nazi government—would not have to receive as many Jewish refugees. Mirroring this in the United States, white supremacists have historically supported the separatist politics of the Nation of Islam. They have seen Black separatism as analogous to the white nationalist "self-determining politic" of the white majoritarian United States.[7] Of course, these logics of racial self-determination do not operate the same in reverse. Their endorsement of Black separatism is not support for Black liberation but rather an understanding that the self-segregation of the Black community means less labor will be needed to remove racial impurity (non-whiteness) in the actualization of their fully white ethnostate. Richard Spencer recently articulated his identity as a self-proclaimed "white Zionist," stating: "I want us to

6. On December 10, 1942, a report called "The Mass Extermination of Jews in German Occupied Poland" published by the Polish Ministry of Foreign Affairs-in exile was presented to United Nations member-states. The sixteen-page report provided details "concern[ed] the mass extermination of Jews in Polish territories occupied by Germany."

7. "Self-determining" in the context of white nationalism is placed in scare quotes because the need for white liberation and self-determination within global white supremacy is spurious.

have a secure homeland for us and ourselves. Just like you want a secure homeland in Israel."[8] This represents the shared logics of colonization (see, for example, the way that the white Ashkenazi Jewish minority comprise Israel's power structure) and an ideological alignment between Zionism and U.S. white nationalism. Israeli state politics revolve, ultimately, around the removal and subjugation of the Palestinian people, beginning with the Nakba. The continuation of settler colonial development in Israel has translated into land expropriation, housing demolition, construction of settlements (contravening international law), ghettoization, and disproportionate state violence against Palestinians. In *Letters to Palestine: Writers Respond to War and Occupation*, Robin D.G. Kelley describes the ways in which this liberatory thought is "not only a narrative of slavery, emancipation, and renewal, but with a language to critique America's racist state since the biblical Israel represented a new beginning." Unfortunately, though, much of Black Zionist thought re-creates the logic of settler colonial entitlements rather than build-

8. "White Nationalist Richard Spencer Tells Israelis that Jews Are 'Over-represented,'" *Times of Israel*, August 17, 2017, www.timesofisrael.com/white-nationalist-richard-spencer-tells-israelis-that-jews-are-over-represented.

ing an incisive and critical foundation upon which to critique settler colonialism and build/repair Afro-diasporic
relationships outside of that model. If land-based reparations were to be actualized for Black people in the United
States, models for land-based liberation that are not both
mindful and critical of settler colonialism would perpetuate the expropriation of land from Indigenous communities still fighting to assert their sovereignties. Black
American land politics cannot simply be built on top of
centuries-old exterminatory settler logic of Indigenous removal and genocide. Rather, the actualization of truly liberated land can only come about through dialogue and co-
conspiratorial work with Native communities and a shared
understanding of land use outside of capitalistic models of
ownership.

Black land politics are also crucial in understanding the
threats posed by climate change resulting from capitalism's ethos of growth for the sake of growth and extraction
for the sake of accumulation. The incessant need to extract
resources is not limited to the United States or to capitalism, though the United States leads this particular fray.
There is nothing too sacred to be consumed or too rare to
leave untouched. The natural world is being treated as an
infinite pool of supplies, as if its resources were immedi-

ately replaceable and the degradation reversible. In the meantime, the reigning capitalists have already begun searching for new lands to retreat to and colonize because even they know that their economic system is headed toward destruction. This will occur first in the Global South. Resources will be expended until there is nothing left to take.

Freshwater shortages, deforestation, and dangerous expansion of industry threaten food supplies the world over. Inevitably, resource scarcity and the demise of agriculture will lead to conflicts of increasing scale. When all is said and done, we cannot eat diamonds, gold, coltan, or oil. Competition over remaining resources is already causing conflicts, which, given their locations in the Global South, are infuriatingly treated by many people as natural or "inherent" to the populations residing in these regions. The planet cannot sustain a violent system relentlessly demanding more and more consumption. Claudia von Werlhof notes:

> Under our system, anything subject to natural limitations appears as inherently scarce. Capital is insatiable. It needs more than nature has; it needs infinitely more. Hence, anything subject to natural limitations, "scarce" in the system's terms and,

moreover, anything which is an indispensable precondition as a means of production for further production, must—in an economic system such as ours—not only be under some kind of control but be brought under *monopolistic* control.[9]

Those of us who are treated as natural commodities, particularly Black people (and more particularly the wombs of cisgender Black women), must see our inextricable link to the environment. Land-based politics grounded in a sustained and nurturing relationship with the natural world and in protecting nature is a means of protecting ourselves. If humanity continues on its trajectory of environmental degradation, the destruction of countless animal species, including our own, is inevitable.

Afro-descended people have historically been compared to simians.[10] One can identify the very Black lament that

9. Maria Mies, Veronika Bennholdt-Thomsen, and Claudia von Werlhof, *Women: The Last Colony* (London: Zed Books, 1988), 101.

10. The Negro-simian analogy is a staple of scientific racist rhetoric. In *Notes on the State of Virginia* (1785) Thomas Jefferson wrote: "Whether the black of the negro resides in the reticular membrane between the skin and scarf-skin, or in the scarf-skin itself; whether it proceeds from the color of the blood, the color of the bile, or from that of some other secretion, the difference is fixed in nature, and is as real as if its seat and cause were better known to us. And is this difference of no

we have been "treated like animals," whether in the cages of the carceral state or within white supremacist America writ large. We are commodified and transformed into something over which white supremacy is able to assert authority and claim ownership. In the not-too-distant past, zoos sometimes displayed African people as if they were something less than human, if not less than animal, if not *less than both*. Displayed as a kind of social and biological oddity, Ota Benga, a Mbuti pygmy from what is now the Democratic Republic of Congo, was purchased from slave traders and eventually displayed in the Monkey House at the Bronx Zoo in 1906.[11] We still do not fit the white hu-

---

importance? Is it not the foundation of a greater or less share of beauty in the two races? Are not the fine mixtures of red and white, the expressions of every passion by greater or less suffusions of color in the one, preferable to that eternal monotony, which reigns in the countenances, that immovable veil of black which covers all the emotions of the other race? *Add to these, flowing hair, a more elegant symmetry of form, their own judgment in favor of the whites, declared by their preference of them, as uniformly as is the preference of the Oran-ootan for the black women over those of his own species. The circumstance of superior beauty, is thought worthy attention in the propagation of our horses, dogs, and other domestic animals; why not in that of man?"* [our emphasis].

11. Phillips Verner Bradford and Harvey Blume, *Ota Benga: The Pygmy in the Zoo* (New York: St. Martins Press, 1992), 172–175.

man default projected into our psyches through the news, public education, pop culture, and virtually all other media we digest within white supremacist society. Climate change and its ravages are not waiting for us to fix our patterns of destructive behavior. We are the only ones who can stop our own causal actions, and this will require more than just words. The responsibility for reversing the harm humans have caused to the environment does not rest with the oppressed peoples of the world who have contributed to it least. Yet the responsible parties refuse to mobilize resources to mitigate the havoc they have wreaked. With that said, our work to end the deterioration of nature must be understood as a necessary and inseparable component of a global anticapitalist movement. What we have come to know as "environmentalism" in the United States and the Western world is entrenched in the saviorism inherent to whiteness, but the most critical environmental politics and frontline resisters to climate change emerge from communities in the Global South, particularly indigenous communities.

These communities in the Global South and those most oppressed in the Global North have become the primary victims of climate change. In line with oppressive victim-blaming, Western capitalists blame environmental problems on "overpopulation" and resource consumption by poor Black and Brown people. Rather than re-evaluating the pace of resource extraction and unsustainable environmental practices, they resort to the sinister logic of Malthusianism.[12] In the name of "family planning" and "empowering Third World women," environmentalists often seek to curb the growing populations of the Global South, despite clear evidence that industrialized Western states are largely responsible for global environmental damage. In *Ecofeminism*, Maria Mies and Vandana Shiva assert,

> That industrialization, technological progress and the affluent life-style of the developed nations have precipitated the acceleration of environmental degradation worldwide can no longer be ignored. The main threats are: 1) degradation of land

12. The Malthusian trap, as offered by Thomas Malthus, states that while new technologies will improve the global standard of living, increased access to resources will be a boon to population growth and the eventual overpopulation will lead to a net shortage of resources. The response to this concern of overpopulation, namely in response to individuals perceived to be consuming more than their "fair share" of resources (e.g., people dependent upon charity, poor and disabled people, and nonwhite people), is generally policy to ensure non-growth or a population plateau. Historically these solutions have frequently included sterilization (as manifested through global health or domestic policy) or other ways of incentivizing individuals—always poor and nonwhite—to have fewer children.

(for example, desertification, salination, loss of arable land); 2) deforestation, mainly of tropical forests; 3) climate change, due to the destruction of the ozone layer; and 4) global warming, due mainly to increasing rates of carbon dioxide and other gaseous emissions. But instead of looking into the root causes of these threats which it is feared are approaching catastrophic thresholds, they are today almost universally attributed to a single cause: population growth. Not only the affluent North and dominant political and economic interests but UN organizations also subscribe to this view.[13]

The culturally imperialist and patriarchal view Mies and Shiva describe asserts itself in the lives of the people already subjugated globally by the whims of capital. By furthering the intention of a racialized domination of women and their bodies, capitalist systems are able to maintain white supremacist patriarchy for their own social, political, and economic gain while also evading responsibility for the harm they cause. Mies and Shiva continue:

Population growth is not a cause of the environmental crisis but one aspect of it, and both are related to resource alienation and destruction of livelihoods, first by colonialism and then continued by Northern-imposed models of maldevelopment....

13. Maria Mies and Vandana Shiva, *Ecofeminism* (London: Zed Books, 2014), 277.

What is also ignored in this "carrying capacity" discourse is the history of colonial intervention into people's reproductive behavior. This intervention was initially motivated, as in Europe, by the need for more disposable labour, labour freed from subsistence activities and forced to work productively on plantations, farms, roads, in mines and so on for the benefit of foreign capital.[14]

Mies and Shiva determine that "it might then well be more fruitful to directly address the roots of the problem: the exploitative world market system which produces poverty. Giving people rights and access to resources so that they can generate sustainable livelihoods is the only solution to environmental destruction and the population growth that accompanies it."[15] When we think of the hurricanes, earthquakes, tsunamis, typhoons, and all the different forces of nature that have destroyed our communities and taken people's lives, we should be inspired to counter *all* racial capitalist forces that exacerbate natural disaster, from climate change to the racist nature of emergency response. In *Stormy Weather: Katrina and the Politics of Disposability*, Henry Giroux describes the moral failure of the George W. Bush administration in respond-

14. Ibid., 285.
15. Ibid.

ing to the hurricane's aftermath. He notes how the botched relief effort prolonged the suffering of already vulnerable New Orleans residents and made evident the clear prioritization of certain human lives over others and how the city became a "petri dish for the forces of neoliberalism."[16] From the images of survival theft (or "looting") and Black abandonment in the Superdome to the presence of Blackwater contractors providing property protection to the wealthy residents who were able to evacuate, the new era of disposability was made chillingly apparent. Giroux writes,

> As Hurricane Katrina vividly illustrated, the decline of the social state along with the rise of massive inequality increasingly bar whole populations from the rights and guarantees accorded to fully fledged citizens of the republic, who are increasingly rendered disposable, and left to fend for themselves in the face of natural or human-made disasters. This last challenge is difficult, for here we must connect the painful dots between the crisis in the Gulf Coast and that "other" Gulf crisis in the Middle East; we must connect the dots between images of US soldiers stand-

16. The excerpt from Giroux's *Stormy Weather* was reprinted in a *Truthout* article from September 8, 2015 entitled "Revisiting Katrina: Racist Violence and the Politics of Disposability," http://www.truth-out.org/opinion/item/32629-revisiting-hurricane-katrina-racist-violence-and-the-politics-of-disposability.

ing next to tortured Iraqis forced to assume the additional in-
dignity of a dog leash to images of bloated bodies floating in
the toxic waters that overwhelmed New Orleans city streets after five long days of punctuated government indifference to the
suffering of some of its citizen populations.[17]

This system was not designed *for* us, it was built *on top* of
us. Our destruction is built into it, but our liberation can
be built from its downfall. It is here that finding the re-
silience of anticapitalist politics in ourselves and applying
them to nature and the environment will guide us *naturally*. We are not in need of a perfect sectarian model of
how to accomplish the building of new anticapitalist communities. That much will be worked out on individual bases
according to when, where, and who is building. What we
need now is to educate ourselves and our communities to
the point that this common goal is understood.

■

Saidiya Hartman writes in "The Terrible Beauty of the
Slum": "Better the fields and the shotgun houses and the
dusty towns and the interminable cycle of credit and debt,
better this than black anarchy."[18] The slum, the ghetto, the

17. Henry A. Giroux, "Revisiting Katrina."
18. Saidiya Hartman, "The Terrible Beauty of the Slum," *Brick*, July
28, 2017, https://brickmag.com/the-terrible-beauty-of-the-slum.

reservation, the internment camp, and other classed and racialized zones of nonbeing have all been used as spaces within which nonwhite life has been relegated and regulated within American necropolitical structures. "Necropolitics" describes the capacity of the state to dictate who lives and who dies: who is understood as having a right or claim to life and who is relegated to inhumanity and social death. Achille Mbembe asks: "But under what practical conditions is the right to kill, to allow to live, or to expose to death exercised? Who is the subject of this right?"[19] Every space inhabited by blackness, particularly Black people living on society's margins, is a space to which Black life is relegated to die, a space that is visible but is impossible to understand and even offensive to the sensibilities of white people. Urban spaces previously deemed "dangerous" and "unlivable" by white people have suddenly become desirable through urbanization, movement within and between cities, and the continuation of settler enclosure. As a result, these spaces are undergoing cataclysmic changes. Waves of gentrification are displacing Black people from these spaces and into more affordable areas. Black working-class existence is becoming increasingly suburbanized, and this can be attributed at least in part to

19. Achille Mbembe, "Necropolitics." *Public Culture* 15, no. 1 (2003): 11–40.

"broader indirect process[es] caused by exclusionary mechanisms such as the decreasing accessibility and affordability of inner-urban neighborhoods"—that is, gentrification.[20] The violence of gentrification mimics other violent displacements of capitalism. It is not a new form of colonization but rather a continuation of settler colonial dispossession in an urban setting. With raced and classed demographic shifts in urban spaces, there is an accompanying shift in the nature of policing as the state seeks to protect incoming residents who tend to be of higher socioeconomic status than those comprising long-existing communities. Neighborly tensions are buffered by the state. The San Francisco–based Anti-Eviction Mapping Project used 311 calls (for nonemergency services) as one means of measuring these interactions within San Francisco neighborhoods. A study it conducted indicates a steep increase in 311 calls between 2009 and 2014, particularly in the city's most heavily gentrified areas.[21] According to the study, over half of all 311 calls were about public passageway cleaning or graffiti. "Of the more than one million 311 calls, 402,184

20. Cody Hochstenbach and Sako Musterd, "Gentrification and the Suburbanization of Urban Poverty: Changing Urban Geographies through Boom and Bust Periods," *Urban Geography* (2016): 1–28.

21. "311 Reports in SF by Neighborhood 2008–2016," Anti-Eviction Mapping Project, www.antievictionmappingproject.net/311.html.

were about street and sidewalk cleaning, 109,999 were for graffiti on public property and 94,619 for graffiti on private property."[22] There are distinct relationships between gentrification and social cleansing: clear correlations between the entry of new residents into urban spaces and corresponding politics of the pricing out and displacement of long-existing residents and communities and the removal of undesirable aesthetics and behaviors (through, for example, imposed restrictions on loitering and noise).[23] While it is

22. Adam Hudson. "How Punitive and Racist Policing Enforces Gentrification in San Francisco." *Truthout*, April 24, 2017, www.truth-out .org/news/item/30392-how-punitive-and-racist-policing-enforces-gentri fication-in-san-francisco.

23. Black churches have frequently been targeted during gentrification processes, and, because these churches have been historical centerpieces of Black communities, these interactions have indelible effects on how new community relations are formed. In 2015, for example, Oakland's Pleasant Grove Baptist Church, a predominately Black church that has been in its neighborhood for sixty-five years, was slapped with over $3,500 in fines. It was served an advisory letter by the City of Oakland because the neighboring residents filed noise complaints claiming that the overly loud choir practice "may constitute a public nuisance due to its impact to the use and quiet enjoyment of the surrounding community's property." Per the Urban Displacement Project at the University of California at Berkeley, that particular church sits in an area that has been rapidly gentrifying (characterized by residential displacement, the influx of new residents, and skyrocketing rent costs and housing prices) over the past decade.

impossible to know exactly who is making calls and about what, from well-documented patterns of gentrification and the frequently hostile relationships between new residents and long-time residents we can reasonably infer that many of these calls about are made by these relatively affluent new residents offended by the visual "blight" of homelessness/houselessness and vandalism (though much of the "urban graffiti," in fact, consists of both new and longstanding mural projects). These calls comprise what is referred to as order-maintaining policing, "the intervention and suppression of behavior that threatens to be offensive, that threatens to disturb the public peace, or that comes from conflicts among individuals that are public in nature." According to the "broken windows" theory of policing, first introduced by criminologists James Q. Wilson and George L. Kelling in 1982,

At the community level, disorder and crime are usually inextricably linked, in a kind of developmental sequence. Social psychologists and police officers tend to agree that if a window in a building is broken and is left unrepaired, all the rest of the windows will soon be broken. This is as true in nice neighborhoods as in rundown ones. Window-breaking does not necessarily occur on a large scale because some areas are inhabited by determined window-breakers whereas others are populated by window-lovers; rather, one unrepaired broken window is a signal that no one cares, and so breaking more windows costs nothing.[24]

These literally and figuratively broken windows signal the impending breakdown of a community in question: that "a stable neighborhood of families who care for their homes, mind each other's children, and confidently frown on unwanted intruders can change, in a few years or even a few months, to an inhospitable and frightening jungle."[25] Never mind that the abandonment of buildings and the degradation of urban infrastructure is frequently a result of municipal neglect or the migration or shutdown of urban industries. According to "broken windows" logic, it is necessary to maintain order through a hyper-surveillance and regulation of seemingly deteriorating areas, which just so happen to be predominately poorer communities and communities of color. Order is accordingly "maintained" by arresting criminals, though this often translates into the state arresting and filling jails and prisons with low-level nonviolent offenders and punishing people for their poverty and precarity. Homelessness is criminalized through laws pro-

24. George L. Kelling and James Q. Wilson. "Broken Windows: The Police and Neighborhood Safety," *Atlantic*, March 1982, 29–38.
25. Ibid.

hibiting loitering or sitting, eating, sleeping, or panhandling in public spaces. White supremacist hierarchies have long established notions of "order," "humanity," and "citizenship." The formation of the system of mass incarceration saw the maintenance of the system of Black slavery despite formal emancipation in 1865. The Thirteenth Amendment of the Constitution declares, "Neither slavery nor involuntary servitude, except as a punishment for crime whereof the party shall have been duly convicted, shall exist within the United States, or any place subject to their jurisdiction." The critical point, of course, is the permission of slavery as punishment for a crime. The state is constitutionally permitted to use incarcerated people for labor approximate to slavery, which drives the criminalization of nonwhite and economically disenfranchised people as so-called threats to public safety. Within these racialized hierarchies criminality is "marked with the same coding as slave captivity, such that, in essence, blackness is enveloped in such distinctions."[26] Through the inextricable linkage of racialized deviance to Black servitude, whiteness becomes "deputized against those who do not magnetize

26. Revolutionary Abolitionist Movement, *Burn Down the American Plantation: Call for a Revolutionary Abolitionist Movement* (Combustion Books, 2017), 6.

bullets."[27] White people are not simply those the state protects and serves: white people are themselves a part of the policing structure, and the notion of public safety cannot be separated from this deep complicity and investment in this form of state violence. This punitive approach to policing and "public protection" is a precedent that long predates the Clinton administration's euphemistic "tough on crime" policy framework, a social cleansing framework built on the targeting—the re-enslavement—of Black offenders. There is little empirical research indicating the efficacy of broken windows policing, but there is increasing research pointing to the spuriousness of the theory, namely in its conflation of causation and correlation by linking disordered public spaces and the existence of crime.[28] On the

27. Frank B. Wilderson III, "The Prison Slave as Hegemony's (Silent) Scandal," *Social Justice* 30, no. 2 (2003): 18–27.

28. See Sampson and Raudenbush's "Systematic Social Observation of Public Spaces: A New Look at Disorder in Urban Neighborhoods." *American Journal of Sociology* 105, no.3 (November 1999), Harcourt and Ludwig's "Broken Windows: New Evidence from New York City and a Five-City Social Experiment," *University of Chicago Law Review* 73 (2006), and Hinkle and Yang's "A New Look into Broken Windows: What Shapes Individuals' Perceptions of Social Disorder?" *Journal of Criminal Justice* Vol. 42, no. 1 (2014): 26–35, for just three different debunkings of Kelling and Wilson's "broken windows" thesis of social disorder.

relationship between policing patterns and societally held racist biases about criminality, Dorothy Roberts writes:

> One of the main tests in American culture for distinguishing law-abiding from lawless people is their race. Many, if not most, Americans believe that Black people are "prone to violence" and make race-based assessments of the danger posed by strangers they encounter [our emphasis]. The myth of Black criminality is part of a belief system deeply embedded in American culture that is premised on the superiority of whites and inferiority of Blacks. Psychological studies show a substantially greater rate of error in cross-racial identifications when the witness is white and the suspect is Black. White witnesses disproportionately misidentify Blacks because they expect to see Black criminals.[29]

To understand geographies of white supremacy—to understand how white supremacy organizes itself across space and through time—is to understand race and the process through which abstract notions of difference are made material. Anti-blackness is not simply ideological or a personally held opinion about the inferiority of Black people. It is

29. Dorothy E. Roberts. "Race, Vagueness, and the Social Meaning of Order-Maintaining Police," *Journal of Criminal Law and Criminology* 89, no. 3 (1999): 775–836.

also structural processes through which resources are unevenly distributed, which in turn informs the material realities of Black communities, often those of deprivation. These spatial stratifications inevitably affect health, as lack of access to high-quality foods drives incidences of nutrition-related illness like Type II diabetes, cardiovascular disease, and malnourishment, and a lack of access to medical care has led to an increase in Black maternal and infant mortality rates. Stratification also affects educational outcomes and physical safety (due to the nature of policing). A notion of effective Black resistance must revolve at least partly around strategies such as resource pooling and community defense, given the state's refusal to provide adequate resources to Black people. To collectively respond to these geographies of white supremacy effectively requires us first to understand ongoing processes of settler colonial displacement through gentrification and racial capitalism's hoarding and inequitable distribution of resources. This allows us to understand community health and its relationship to local environmental conditions (shaped by political decisions), changing demographics, and so on. Developing this wide analysis, particularly in understanding how local politics are inextricably linked to global processes, allows us to connect with other struggles and potential allies across class, ethnicity, and other lines of identity. Attempting to reclaim and repurpose the settler state will not lead to liberation, and it will not provide the kind of urgent material relief so many people desperately need, though electing empathetic officials sometimes can arguably mitigate against harm. Only through a material disruption of these geographies, through the cultivation of Black autonomy, can Black liberation begin to be actualized.

CHAPTER THREE

GROUNDS TO DEFEND ON

Self-defense is of the utmost importance in the United States. If you can't afford to run from what's threatening you and are interested in continuing your existence, you should learn to fight where you stand. It's something that has consistently defined the United States long after the Revolutionary War. The concept of resisting tyrannical government through arms is ingrained in consciousness across the Americas. Nations birthed through fighting and revolutions against colonial empires glorify their histories of resistance and defense. The United States is no exception and certainly praises this aspect of its history. But the history of rebellion against the U.S. project itself is often glossed over as if an inconvenience to the supposed freedoms we enjoy today. Those of us who believe in human rights and equality have to imagine resistance beyond just words, symbolism, and attitudes. Resistance should also carry a realistic outlook that includes a self-defense strategy. History has regularly given us guidelines for doing so.

Consideration and understanding of individual and community self-defense is mandatory for the movements we hope to build and maintain. In this white supremacist society, movements that challenge the status quo are often violently dismissed. Though Black-led resistance has been very effective in challenging and changing conditions, Black people have often paid with our lives. Whenever there is a dominant system that enables or privileges certain groups over others, violence against those considered lesser is increasingly justified by that system, especially against those defying that system. White supremacy has dehumanized Black people to such an extent that killing Black people is not only widely socially acceptable but also a necessary function of anti-Black subjection. Any Black movement that plans on maintaining itself should be prepared to defend itself if and when necessary.

Our opposition should reflect the earliest moments of Native resistance to European settler conquest; the uprisings of enslaved Africans from plantations to Maroons; the Black Power revolutionary movement; and Black gangs that were born of necessity and are often far better organized than those who denounce them would ever give them credit for. The lessons of the past are here for us, should we choose to accept them and build from what they have to offer. The study of the armed struggle of Native people is foundational in creating a sustainable self-defense movement against white supremacist capitalism and those it enables today. Understanding what worked and what did not can be helpful. The past shows that we should be constantly prepared for infinite varieties of conflict.

Self-defense is not violence, it is a means of survival. It cannot be equated with oppression and assault by the powerful structures that thrive because of everyday violence. This is not a sectarian attempt to co-opt death and destruction for our own means, nor is it an attempt to attain power like that which oppresses. Rather it is an understanding of power, privilege, and history. By starting from the moments people first expressed their objection to the U.S. project and working our way through history into the present, we can begin to understand our need for an opposition that embraces and promotes a healthy philosophy of self-defense.

Our resistance against systemic oppression is not new. Rebellions against white supremacist capitalism have happened across racial lines, and Black people have taken part in them from the moment when enslaved Africans arrived on American shores (and even on the ships that transported them across the Atlantic Ocean). These early rejections of white supremacist capitalism set the precedent for many movements to come, including many of the ones we see today that are arguably much less confrontational.

Black resistance across the Americas has laid the foundations for many of the progressive developments in the nations of the Western Hemisphere, from the establishment of the Haitian Republic to the Black movements that would embrace self-defense in the ways that we can appreciate today. Much of the legislation we value, like the Civil Rights Act and the Voting Rights Act, arose from the state's concessions to the civil rights movement and other Black resistance efforts at the time. What many would call "freedoms" in a society that is *not* free are actually cherished but weakening policies relied upon by oppressed people throughout the nation. Policies and laws, which are not permanently secured, helped bring about some progress in areas like education, labor, entertainment, and many aspects of daily life. The desegregation of public spaces and facilities is one such example. These reforms were admissions of guilt for systemic inequality based on race, gender, ethnicity, and other identities. It is important to realize that without Black resistance such progressive developments would never have occurred.

It is true that Black people have been involved in U.S. expansion, usually by force or coercion. However, Black people have always fought against state power too. Interracial coalitions across the United States have relied on Black people. Black and Native coalitions preceded the Revolutionary War and carried common interests so plain that racial boundaries were often broken to reject not only settler interests but also sometimes British interests.[1] Maroons, for example, were communities made up of predominantly enslaved Africans and Indigenous people across the Americas. For centuries, these communities thrived as hubs of resistance, and sometimes they even attracted some white people who understood their marginalization at the hands of the powerful forces battling over their capitalistic and colonial interests. Nat Turner's 1831 slave rebellion is perhaps considered an anomaly during formative years in the nation's political landscape, but many similar uprisings are not as well known. In the same area where Nat Turner's rebellion took place—Southampton County, Virginia—in the Tidewater region of southeastern Virginia and northeastern North Carolina, a series of conspiracies and insurrections against slavery took place between 1790 and 1810. These uprisings were a "product of over 150 years

1. Neal Shirley and Saralee Stafford, *Dixie Be Damned: 300 Years of Insurrection in the American South* (Oakland: AK Press, 2015), 21.

of autonomous activity by slaves, servants, fugitives, and Natives in the area," Neal Shirley and Saralee Stafford write in *Dixie Be Damned*, and "this period of rebellion forever changed the scope of insurrectionary activity under slavery."[2] Not long after Turner's rebellion, enslaved Africans and Native people in Florida engaged in what is arguably the most successful slave rebellion in American history. The launch of the Second Seminole War would provide the foundation for the first emancipation proclamation, decades before Abraham Lincoln's. Led by the likes of John Horse, Osceola, Wild Cat, and King Phillip, Natives, Blacks, and Black Natives fought valiantly alongside one another against the full, unleashed force of the U.S. military. The Black Seminole contingent of this rebellion was complex. Some of the Black people fighting had been enslaved by white owners, while others had been enslaved by Seminoles or had lived with them. No form of slavery is redeemable or justifiable, but Seminoles offered enslaved Africans more rights and sometimes integration into the tribe, and they would fight alongside one another against white conquest and enslavement. The fierce fight-

2. Ibid., 17.

ing of those dubbed "Indian-negroes" is well documented in U.S. history. In 1837 U.S. Army general Thomas Jesup wrote, "The two races are rapidly approximating; they are identified in interests and feelings.... Should the Indians remain in this territory, the Negroes among them will form a rallying point for runaway Negroes from the adjacent states; and should they remove, the fastnesses of the country would be immediately occupied by negroes."[3]

In 1836, when General Jesup had realized that he could not effectively defeat this uprising, he had declared, "This, you may be assured, is a negro, not an Indian war; and if it be not speedily put down, the south will feel the effects of it on their slave population before the end of the next season."[4] And with that, Jesup issued the first emancipation proclamation, which stated that "All Negroes the property of the Seminole ... who ... delivered themselves up to the Commanding Officer of the Troops should be free."[5] This first and largely unrecognized proclamation of Black emancipation was secured through armed struggle and

3. Quoted in Adam Wasserman, *A People's History of Florida 1513–1876: How Africans, Seminoles, Women, and Lower Class Whites Shaped the Sunshine State* (Oakland Park, FL: A. Wasserman, 2009), 205, 206.

4. Ibid., 183.

5. Ibid., 222.

an unrelenting multiyear battle for Blacks' right to self-determination. Slave owners who had hoped the military would return those who had escaped with the Seminoles were forced to accept defeat. While this led to momentary optimism on behalf of some Black Seminoles and further compromises around Black and Native emancipation and self-determination, promises made by the state were later reversed or broken, as most agreements with Black and Indigenous communities historically have been. After years of fighting and then engaging in the politics of their day, arguably reformist, they decided to take their fate into their own hands. Black Seminole leader John Horse worked with the state in an effort to appease his adversaries through service, policy change, and negotiation. When he was captured in 1838, he agreed to relocate some of his people in exchange for peace. That relocation compromise would be filled with broken promises. After John Horse worked as a guide and negotiator for the U.S. Army, he saw that the hopes of his people were not being realized through moderate methods. His unsuccessful petitioning for the government to treat the Black Seminoles better was not the end of the matter. The Black Seminole communities were ultimately forced to simultaneously fight and flee, with many settling in Texas, Mexico, and even parts of the Bahamas, among other places. Their communities still exist and serve as examples of ongoing Black resistance.

This frequently overlooked history illustrates some lessons of revolution, repression, and reform. The Black Seminole movements necessarily adjusting to change and state response embodies the anarchism of blackness. The Black Seminoles' repression by the U.S. government and their alienation from certain segments of the Seminole nation demanded that they adapt to reality. In the same way, Black people today are subject to persistent repression and often are alienated from the movements of people of color who are not Black. The Black Seminoles fought, resisted, and retreated when necessary because any attempts at accommodation failed to benefit them in the end. Their statelessness and often deferred, if not excluded, tribal status among the Seminoles locates them in the vortex that is the Black condition, and their unique fight for self-determination highlights the intricacies of Black struggle.

Now caught up in the dialogue of liberalism, many activist communities have largely been lacking a coherent conversation about self-defense. In the liberal history of the civil rights movement, "nonviolence" and Martin Luther King Jr. are the centerpiece, and this is held up as the right way to go about seeking social change. This has manifest frequently during rebellions (derisively called "riots"), often in response to incidents of state violence or extrajudicial killings. From Baltimore to Ferguson, Los Angeles, and wherever there is a Black uprising, the state and its allies attempt to subdue Black people by invoking nonviolence and King, who is conveniently remembered for his civil disobedience but not for his armed guards or gun ownership.

King, Malcolm X (El-Hajj Malik El-Shabazz), Harriet Tubman, W. E. B. Du Bois, Fannie Lou Hamer, Ida B. Wells, and countless other Black leaders employed self-defense in theory as well as praxis to get us to this point. Many of us may relate to the words of the NAACP co-founder Du Bois's response to the Atlanta Race Riot of 1906:

I revered life. I have never killed a bird nor shot a rabbit. I never liked fishing and always let others kill even the chickens which I ate. Nearly all my schoolmates in the South carried pistols. I never owned one. I could never conceive myself killing a human being. But in 1906 I rushed back from Alabama to Atlanta where my wife and six-year old child were living. A mob had raged for days killing Negroes. I bought a Winchester double-barreled shotgun and two dozen rounds of shells filled with buckshot. If a white mob had stepped on the campus where I lived I would without hesitation have sprayed their guts over the grass. They did not come.[6]

Legendary civil rights leader Fannie Lou Hamer was an outspoken advocate of peaceful methods of resistance. Her emphasis on love and morality is far more well known than her thoughts about the possibility of conflict with white supremacists. Hamer once said that hatred "makes us sick and weak," but her politics of love did not contradict her embrace of self-defense. She stated, "I keep a shotgun in every corner of my bedroom and the first cracker even look like he wants to throw some dynamite on my porch won't write his mama again."[7] Hamer and Du Bois are just two examples of Black people who have historically walked the imagined line between promoting self-defense and what we've come to know as nonviolence. Martin Luther King's own writings seem to affirm this balance:

6. W. E. B. Du Bois, *The Autobiography of W.E.B. Du Bois: A Soliloquy on Viewing My Life from the Last Decade of Its First Century* (New York, NY: International Publishers, 1968), 286.

7. Charles E. Cobb Jr., *This Nonviolent Stuff'll Get You Killed: How Guns Made the Civil Rights Movement Possible* (Durham, NC: Duke University Press Books, 2015), 124.

Violence exercised merely in self-defense, all societies, from the most primitive to the most cultured and civilized, accept as moral and legal. The principle of self-defense, even involving weapons and bloodshed has never been condemned.... When the Negro uses force in self-defense he does not forfeit support—he may even win it, by the courage and self-respect it reflects. When he seeks to initiate violence, he provokes questions about the necessity for it, and inevitably is blamed for its consequences. It is unfortunately true that however the Negro acts, his struggle will not be free of violence initiated by his enemies, and he will need ample courage and willingness to sacrifice to defeat this manifestation of violence.[8]

The United States has not been bombed, destabilized, and wrecked—as have the nations whose resources it plunders. It enjoys a relative peace of sorts, absent outright war or bloody conflict that we see around the world. The violence of the state is deeply entrenched within institutions and made invisible by those institutions well enough to deceive many into believing that the life we're familiar with is acceptable. Many may feel that the apparent and relative

8. Martin Luther King Jr., *A Testament of Hope: The Essential Writings and Speeches of Martin Luther King, Jr.* (New York City: Harper Collins, 1990), 33.

peace of a system is comfortable, safe enough to not demand fighting for anything better despite the violence and death built into the system. But the reality of fascist white supremacist violence tells us something very different. We should prepare for individual and collective self-defense, since our turbulent history in the United States warns us this will be needed. Even the most nonconfrontational and compassionate among us should understand that conflict has defined the U.S. project from its inception, through genocidal, xenophobic, and anti-Black violence.

Liberal appropriation and misreading of history attempt to implement respectability politics as defining Black resistance. But it is a myth that our enemies will love us or value us more as people if our appearance and behavior are more respectable—that is, dictated by white (supremacist) liberal sensibilities. This is so common that some young contemporary activists assert that "we are not our grandparents"—as if our grandparents were timid, fearful, and nonconfrontational (so often they were very much the opposite).[9] No honest telling of history will re-

9. In 2016, on social media, ads surfaced for a T-shirt with a message on it that read *"Dear Racism, I'm not my grandparents. Sincerely, These Hands."* The T-shirt raised ire among many for blatantly disregarding the history of self-defense in the Black community, while some chose to defend the message, believing it to be accurate.

veal a complacent Black population that passively took whatever violence was inflicted on them. Even in the face of oppressive law enforcement, a constant for Black people historically, respectability has never deterred self-defense. Ida B. Wells once wrote: "A Winchester rifle should have a place of honor in every black home, and it should be used for that protection which the law refuses to give. When the white man who is always the aggressor knows he runs as great risk of biting the dust every time his Afro-American victim does, he will have greater respect for Afro-American life. The more the Afro-American yields and cringes and begs, the more he has to do so, the more he is insulted, outraged and lynched."[10]

Most of the imagined and circumstantial retelling of the civil rights movement can easily be debunked. Even the nonviolent civil disobediences were far more disruptive and confrontational than public imagination often allows them to be. In his landmark book *Negroes with Guns*, North Carolina NAACP organizer Robert F. Williams challenged the concept and practice of passive nonviolence, which was popular among activists like himself at the time. His work would later influence Huey P. Newton,

---

10. Ida B. Wells, *Southern Horrors: Lynch Law in All Its Phases* (Auckland, New Zealand: Floating Press, 2014), 36.

who would become a founding member of the Black Panther Party along with Bobby Seale. Williams wrote, "The stranglehold of oppression cannot be loosened by a plea to the oppressor's conscience. Social change in something as fundamental as racist oppression involves violence. You cannot have progress here without violence and upheaval, because it's a struggle for survival for one and a struggle for liberation for the other. Always the powers in command are ruthless and unmerciful in defending their position and their privileges. This is not an abstract rule to be meditated upon by Americans."[11]

While we may choose not to limit or misrepresent the diversity of our struggle by explicitly naming ourselves as "anarchists," we should nevertheless cultivate an internationalist framework and draw inspiration from movements for sovereignty and autonomy both domestically and globally. Black anarchist Lorenzo Kom'boa Ervin explains:

Two features of a new mass movement must be the intention of creating dual power institutions to challenge the state, along with the ability to have a grassroots autonomist movement that can take advantage of a pre-revolutionary situation to go all the way. Dual power means that you organize a number of col-

11. Williams, *Negroes with Guns*, 72.

lectives and communes in cities and town[s] all over North America, which are, in fact, liberated zones, outside of the control of the government. Autonomy means that the movement must be truly independent and a free association of all those united around common goals, rather than membership as the result of some oath or other pressure.[12]

This model of organizing shies away from hierarchies, cultism, and performative militancy; it prioritizes people over cults of personality and traditional models of leadership that are highly centralized. Ervin also writes:

As Blacks and other oppressed peoples of color, we are living through some of the most perilous times in both American and world history. The white empire is declining, but in its desperation to cling to power, we face police murder and brutality, mass imprisonment of youth of color, racial profiling, degrading poverty and unemployment, repressive anti-terrorist legislation and new wars of conquest and yet we do not hear the voices of organized peoples of color in their millions in North America. Instead, we are part of "someone else's agenda" or "someone else's political organization," but it is time now to

12. Lorenzo Kom'boa Ervin, *Anarchism and the Black Revolution*, Anarchist Library, 1993. https://theanarchistlibrary.org/library/lorenzo-kom-boa-ervin-anarchism-and-the-black-revolution#toc33.

build our own and speak for ourselves. We must not only demand our "rights" in a Western capitalist society, but fight to build a new world.[13]

It is not sufficient to simply center blackness in our understanding of resistance to subjugation. We must also explicitly name different gendered and sexual identities within blackness. Any truly liberatory politics must speak to the unique needs and vulnerability of Black women and girls, particularly Black queer and transgender women and girls. There are ongoing murders of Black trans women across the country (and trans women around the world) because women's safety is a non-priority of the state and because patriarchal gender structures are ultimately grounded in transmisogyny.[14] Black women are also being hunted,

13. Lorenzo Kom'boa Ervin, *Anarchism and the Black Revolution* (Denver: P&L Printing, 2011), 104.

14. We understand patriarchy as ultimately revolving around transmisogyny because, through the deliberate mis-gendering of trans women and the invalidation of their womanhood, transmisogyny serves as a correction for manhood and masculinity. Through this violent structural understanding, trans women are perceived through violent tropes, which ultimately justifies the violence and exclusion they experience (in, for example, trans-exclusionary feminist spaces that perceive trans women as somehow "appropriating" or attempting to enter spaces to violate "real"

but this hunting season (unlike the open season on Black men) is grossly under-addressed because of the frequent de-gendering of antiracist politics, the invisibilization of Black women through diversity language like "women and people of color" that overlooks the intersections of race and gender, the erasure of Black women within "women of color," and understandings of how state violence against Black people focuses on the humiliation and emasculation and almost sole targeting of cisgender black men. A politic of self-defense cannot ignore the intersections of white supremacist state violence and its manifestations of intracommunal violence against Black women (trans and cis), as well as other members of the Black community who are marginalized beyond their blackness.

Black feminism says that the forces of sexism and (trans)misogyny, classism, and racism are inextricably linked in a mutually constitutive web of oppressions and

women). This gendered violence, of course, is compounded by raced and classed identities and locations. It is unsurprising that the majority of trans women of color that have been killed in 2017 have been black trans women. On media depictions of trans women, Julia Serano writes about "deceptive" and "pathetic" archetypes in *Whipping Girl: A Transsexual Woman on Sexism and the Scapegoating of Femininity* (Berkeley, CA: Seal Press, 2007).

domination.[15] Within this tradition, of course, is Kimberlé
Crenshaw's "intersectionality,"[16] building from the intel-
lectual legacy of Black lesbian feminists and even nineteenth-century Black feminist works such as writings by
Anna Julia Cooper.[17] Black feminism too grounds political
understandings (and anticapitalist critiques) in embodied
knowledge and lived experiences, and it also has the potential to present non-essentialized and non-biologized critiques of the position of Black womanhood within history,
a kind of useful historical revisionism highlighting racial
capitalism's violence against Black women and Black na-

15. Patricia Hill Collins. *Black Feminist Thought: Knowledge, Consciousness, and the Politics of Empowerment* (New York: Routledge,
2000).

16. Kimberlé Crenshaw, "Mapping the Margins: Intersectionality,
Identity Politics, and Violence Against Women of Color," *Stanford Law
Review* 43, no. 6 (Jul., 1991): 1241–1229.

17. Crenshaw, "Mapping the Margins." See also: Barbara Smith's ed-
ited anthology *Home Girls: A Black Feminist Anthology* (New York:
Kitchen Table, Women of Color Press, 1983); *All the Women are White,
All the Blacks are Men, But Some of Us are Brave* by Gloria T. Hull, Patricia Bell Scott, and Barbara Smith (New York: The Feminist Press at
the City University of New York, 1982); Audre Lorde's *Sister Outsider*
(Berkeley: Crossing Press, 1984); and *Women, Race, and Class* (New
York: Vintage Books, 1983) for pre-Crenshaw classic Black feminist
works that share in this framework.

tionalism's frequent exclusion of them. Black feminism responds to the racist exclusion of Black women from "women's issues"—safety, deservedness, agency and autonomy, and classed oppression. Understanding Black women's subjugation by the state means understanding raced and gendered labor extraction, and Black feminism is useful for understanding the functioning of capitalism and for undermining the legitimacy of this anti-Black settler state.

Understanding Black women's subjugation means understanding the ways that Black women's labor was central to the development of the capitalist state and the American slaveocracy. Sarah Haley's *No Mercy Here* narrates how gendered anti-blackness formed the cornerstone of Jim Crow modernity, which then paved the way for the contemporary system of mass incarceration that we have today. Haley's book compares the hyper-imprisonability of black women's gender deviance and the redeemability of white femininity and shows how these constructs were made material through judicial sentencing that enforced Black women's subjection. Black women were understood to be as strong as men and were used frequently for manual labor in the fields, whereas white women were only employed in fields as punishment for particularly bad behavior. Haley writes that in 1893, "Black men were 1.4 times more likely than white men to be arrested in Atlanta, while Black women were 6.4 times more likely than white women to be arrested." That year, "Black male youth were three times more likely to be arrested than young white males while young Black girls were nineteen times more likely to be arrested than their white female counter parts."[18] The normativity and virtuosity of white women is made concrete through the deliberate singling out and punishment of Black women and girls. It is also through the tripled labor (domestic, industrial, and sexual—euphemistically called "social reproduction"—labor as Black women's bodies become playthings for white prison guards) and the male-approximate punishment of the chain gang that Black women were further and further excluded from womanhood. White women ultimately became exempted from chain gang labor, the only demographic to be protected from carceral punishment in this way, codifying a race-gender structure revolving around the protection of white womanhood and rooted in anti-Black criminalizations.

When we look at contemporary antiracist politics, Black humanity and personhood continue to be filtered and evaluated through the white liberal imagination. In "Against

18. Sarah Haley, *No Mercy Here: Gender, Punishment, and the Making of Jim Crow Modernity* (Chapel Hill: University of North Carolina Press, 2016), 30.

Innocence: Race, Gender, and the Politics of Safety" Jackie Wang asserts a frame for understanding Black personhood and victimization. A notion of innocence is a precondition for launching antiracist support campaigns, she says, and such campaigns arise only when Black people are able to pass tests of moral purity.[19] So we can, for example, largely agree that Tamir Rice was egregiously victimized because he was a child. The outpouring of empathy was due to his youth (as was the corroboration of his claim to innocence via surveillance footage), the same as with Aiyana Stanley-Jones. But Mike Brown failed the test because he may have committed strongarm robbery (despite robbery not being a capital offense), and Darren Wilson's testimony added to the process of what Frank B. Wilderson III refers to as "niggerization."[20]

19. Jackie Wang, "Against Innocence: Race, Gender, and the Politics of Safety," *LIES: A Journal of Materialist Feminism* 1 (2012): 145–171.

20. Frank B. Wilderson III, "Grammar & Ghosts: The Performative Limits of American Freedom," *Theatre Survey* 50, no. 1 (2009): 123. In Cornel West, "Niggerization," *Atlantic*, November 2007, www.the atlantic.com/magazine/archive/2007/11/niggerization/306285, West describes "niggerization" as "neither simply the dishonoring and devaluing of black people nor solely the economic exploitation and political disenfranchisement of them. It is also the wholesale attempt to impede democratization—to turn potential citizens into intimidated, fearful, and helpless subjects."

Similarly, we did not see an outpouring of empathy and support for CeCe McDonald, a Black trans woman who was convicted of second-degree manslaughter after killing an attacker who violently confronted her with racist and transmisogynistic language and smashed a drink against her face, clearly a case of self-defense. She accepted a plea bargain of forty-one months in prison in June 2012 and served nineteen months in two different men's facilities before being released in January 2014. Given the epidemic of assault and murder of Black trans women, was her defensive violence not warranted? What makes her less "innocent" than, for example, Marissa Alexander, who fired a warning shot after her husband attacked and threatened to kill her? There was far more outcry about the gendered implications of women invoking "Stand Your Ground" laws than about the perfectly reasonable use of violence in response to the assault of a Black trans woman, perhaps because in the case of Alexander, white liberals (particularly white feminists) were able to apply the carceral feminist logic of protecting the world from scary racialized men that sits at the root of so many implicitly racialized anti–domestic violence and intimate partner violence interventions. (It is important for us to note our steadfast support of both women, and the contrast of their cases was

not intended to indicate our personal perceptions of one woman being "more innocent" or "more deserving" of support than the other, but rather the disparate nature of public solidarity given their specific contexts.)

Where so many antiracist logics—even ones emerging from radical spaces—appeal to innocence, we continue to rely on the logic of the white imagination and draw upon exceptional cases to buttress our arguments. But ultimately, in doing so, we inadvertently affirm illegitimate modes of governance and social regulation in an ultimately illegitimate state.[21] Reliance upon empathy fails to produce politics that unequivocally affirm black humanity. In doling out our own judgments of innocence, we fail to articulate the state's relationship to (and production of) blackness. "Innocence" defenses can only be flawed because the disciplinary systems erected around us—the ghetto, the

21. On defense campaigns and abolitionist organizing, Mariame Kaba writes: "Of course, defense campaigns are most effective as abolitionist strategies when they are framed in a way that speaks to the need to abolish prisons in general. The campaign cannot be framed by a message such as: 'This is the one person who shouldn't be in prison, but everyone else should be.' Rather, individual cases should be framed as emblematic of the conditions faced by thousands or millions who should also be free." ("Free Us All," *New Inquiry*, May 8, 2017, https://thenewinquiry.com/free-us-all).

plantation, the prison, the colony—define us solely through our criminality, deviance, and an ongoing existence as both capital and a heavily subsidized labor force for the state. The issue is not to improve our ability to convincingly argue the innocence of brutalized and slain Black individuals immortalized through hashtags. We occupy a criminal subject position that cannot be shifted by appeals to white emotion. The state does not simply produce anti-Black systems, it *is* anti-blackness.

Wang further discusses "zones of intelligibility," spaces of being and residing that are understandable to white people. Trayvon Martin and Oscar Grant, she writes, were both murdered in places intelligible to white imaginations, a gated community and a public transportation station, respectively. Still, violence has occurred in "alternate universes"—the slave ship, the hood, prisons, and anywhere in public but at the hands of the state. What happens when Blacks possess an unintelligible identity? We are forced to perform the dehumanizing mental gymnastics of appealing to white notions of innocence and perfect victimhood. Affirming the legitimacy of self-defense is a refusal to entertain the idea that Black people have only a conditional right to life. It is the embrace of a legacy of community self-determination by any means necessary.

Like the abusive entity that it is, white supremacist oppression conditions those it oppresses to tolerate violence for the educational purposes of *all* its white beneficiaries. Through dialogue and discussion, protest and pain, and brutality and death, those oppressed by white supremacy are supposed to work to educate their oppressors on how not to oppress them: to risk death in order to show our oppressors we are not deserving of their violence. Invoking many Black leaders of the past who have been redefined by white imaginations, white liberal politics suggests that we should be brutalized and possibly killed as martyrs for our cause as well as for the betterment of white America. White supremacist logic has been so convincing that we oppressed people have largely come to believe that self-defense itself is violence. Even more unsettling is the fact that many oppressed people get caught up in white centrist politics as a means of liberation, as if anyone or anything that oppresses us will guide us to rid ourselves of oppression.

Centrist politics look for a reasonable middle between fascistic domination and resistance against it. This liberal accommodationism relies on the illusion of two logical sides. Violent conflicts are reduced to mere disagreements, as if one side's dehumanization of another is just a difference of opinion. Oppression becomes softened, in discussions at least, by the farcical centrist propaganda that it should be negotiated rather than abolished. With this in mind, we must clarify that violence against us is intolerable under any circumstance. But just as violence against us is intolerable, so is violence against women, gender non-conforming people, and queer and trans people within our communities. It's not that the misleading narratives of "Black on Black crime" justify the violence against us from outside our community, but by protecting those who are most vulnerable within our communities we will be strengthening our defense against *any* outside aggressions.

Black women are doubly and uniquely exploited on the basis of both their blackness and their womanhood. The enslavement that concretized the conditions of the anarchistic nature of blackness in the United States sometimes runs parallel to other oppressions and sometimes intersects with them. Black women's enslavement and underpaid and undervalued productive and reproductive labor highlight the abusive exploitation of white supremacist capitalism that reigns over us. Through patriarchal domination, women are understood not as complete humans but as part of nature, reduced solely to assigned gender roles like domestic labor as well as the ability to produce and rear children. At the same time, women's ability to bear and produce children is discounted as natural in the sense that it is stripped of its labor value and the resources that it produces: the workforce, representing both labor and potential capital itself. Giving birth is "going into labor," but it is not a paid job because it is understood as the natural responsibility of women. In *Women: The Last Colony*, Maria Mies writes, "One of the greatest obstacles to women's liberation is that activities are still interpreted as purely physiological functions, comparable to those of other mammals, and lying outside the sphere of conscious human influence."[22]

The American ethno-state has been and continues to be lauded by white supremacists as a model for its exclusion of nonwhites.[23] This is partly why we argue that Black people are non-citizens in the United States, even though most of us were born here and our families have existed here for generations. Our hyper-exploitability is linked to our societal location as the descendants of slaves in the "aftermath" of a chattel trade that has not yet ended. Blackness

22. Mies, Bennholdt-Thomsen, and von Werlhof, *Women: The Last Colony*, 74.

23. In *Mein Kampf*, Adolf Hitler wrote that the United States was the "one State which manifests at least some modest attempts that show a better appreciation of how things ought to be done." Hitler's praise of the U.S. genocidal conquest and oppression of nonwhites continues to inspire and animate white supremacists to this day.

and the oppressive efforts to undo Black humanity link us as a people to slavery, and blackness is in turn seen as the essence of enslaveability. Our labor and our beings are seen as "nature," "objects to be appropriated, exploited, and destroyed."[24] This view of blackness positions Black people as being a supposedly endless resource, the same way capitalism treats commodifiable natural resources like wood or water. Claudia von Werlhof makes another intricate connection in the description of women as nature:

> Women have been assigned to "nature" precisely because they have been deprived of their nature, because, un-naturally, they are not permitted to control their natural capabilities. The universal drive to turn women into "nature" is the absolute economic precondition of our present-day mode of production as distinct from its predecessors. The diverse forms of patriarchal control over women seen in preceding systems, such as exchange and theft of women, marriage regulations and kinship systems, never attained the intensity, extremes and absoluteness of those operating at present, leaving aside a moment of its global extension—a fact unaltered by any seeming "emancipation."[25]

24. Mies, Bennholdt-Thomsen, and von Werlhof, *Women: The Last Colony*, 97.

25. Ibid., 103.

The anarchistic nature of blackness created by white supremacist oppression positions us as things that are exploitable, commodifiable, and enslaveable. By understanding how oppression works to make us less human, if human at all, we can begin to understand certain forms of disorder within our communities. Violence against the most vulnerable in our communities and poverty (lack of resources) are problems that stem from the dominant white belief that Black people *are* a resource and not people with human rights. With the repression of Black social movements, the likes of gangs and other black organizations that are considered illegitimate grew into what are largely designated problems in our communities today. In "Blackstone Rangers," Gwendolyn Brooks writes:

There they are.
Thirty at the corner.
Black, raw, ready.
Sores in the city
that do not want to heal.
. . . .
Jeff. Gene. Geronimo. And Bop.
They cancel, cure and curry.
Hardly the dupes of the downtown thing
the cold bonbon,

the rhinestone thing. And hardly
in a hurry.
Hardly Belafonte, King,
Black Jesus, Stokely, Malcolm X or Rap.
Bungled trophies.
Their country is a Nation on no map.[26]

Whether or not we accept it, Black Americans who are descendants of enslaved Africans, like the gangs Brooks describes, have largely existed as a nation on no map. Eugene Hairston and Jeff Fort were founding members of the Blackstone Rangers, a gang formed in Chicago in the late 1950s. The Blackstone Rangers (also known as Black P. Stone Nation or BPSN) are an example of the complex history of many gangs in this country. The group looked very different at its founding than it looks today. They once secured funding from the government in the form of an almost million-dollar grant via the Woodlawn Organization to do community work on Chicago's South Side.[27] By using

26. Gwendolyn Brooks, "The Blackstone Rangers," in *The Penguin Anthology of Twentieth-century American Poetry*, ed. Rita Dove (New York: New York, 2011), 186.

27. James Alan McPherson, "Chicago's Blackstone Rangers (I)," *Atlantic*, May 1969, www.theatlantic.com/magazine/archive/1969/05/chicagos-blackstone-rangers-i/305741.

the existing gang structure of the Blackstone Rangers and the Devil's Disciples (now Black Disciples), the hope was to provide employment preparation and motivational services to those targeted. Due to mismanagement, that never happened. The Blackstone Rangers' roots also lie in a Black nationalistic message not unlike like that of the Black Panther Party.

Many gangs, like the Black P. Stones, the Black Guerrilla Family, and the Crips, can trace their history in this way, and these histories directly relate to the necessity of self-defense and community control. If not for the Black Panthers and the Black Power movement, how would today's activists understand and conceptualize self-defense? Despite the movement's inspiring history, these politics are often romanticized and overly, if not impractically, emphasized by many Black nationalists today. The Black Panthers should be appreciated as well as problematized; they should be studied instead of just badly mimicked for the sake of militancy. Any ideology of self-defense must have the will, desire, and support of the communities we claim to represent.

The Black Panther Party's origins trace back to Lowndes County, Alabama, and the Student Nonviolent Coordinating Committee's (SNCC) work registering Black voters. Kwame Ture (formerly known as Stokely Carmichael), who popularized the phrase "Black Power," did some of his most well-known work in Lowndes County. Despite being the overwhelming majority in the county, Black residents were completely under the thumb of ruling whites. For easy identification on voter registration cards, SNCC developed a black panther logo. This logo originally belonged to the Lowndes County Freedom Organization, but it was later adapted by the Black Panther Party for Self-Defense when a Lowndes County pamphlet wound up in the hands of Huey P. Newton and Bobby Seale in Oakland. But the logo and the Black Power message were not all that would inspire them.

Obviously, the white minority in Lowndes County was not happy about the community organizing and mobilization of Black voters. They worked hard to threaten and intimidate the community that was trying to secure representation. Much like today, police could not be depended on to protect Black people, and so movement leaders in Lowndes armed themselves however they could and however they deemed necessary: they carried weapons while they canvassed and organized.[28] Guns were not in short supply because the Black community was already armed,

28. Hasan Kwame Jeffries, *Bloody Lowndes: Civil Rights and Black Power in Alabama's Black Belt* (New York: NYU Press, 2010), 102.

and community members provided them with additional arms. The presence of guns in this regard underscores the history of Black self-defense as well as the local communities' willingness to engage in self-defense. "There was no need for suicidal displays of bravado because everyone in the black community knew of their commitment to armed self-defense."[29] They actively defended themselves against attacks by whites while establishing their own political power, demonstrating their dedication to the cause of universal Black suffrage.

The self-defense organizing in Selma was not limited to one particular entity or group, and it focused on necessity rather than showy militancy. When our forebears began to arm themselves, it wasn't necessarily because they believed in the Founding Fathers' promise of the "right to bear arms." Rather, the only thing white America had ever promised Black America was violence. Guns were a way to possibly protect oneself from that violence. But the promise of the "right to bear arms," like the rest of the U.S. Constitution, does not functionally apply to anyone who is not a white man, just as the original definition of citizenship did not apply to anyone other than white landowning men.

29. Ibid., 103.

Black people's "right" to anything in the United States is an abstraction: the founders denied Black people, free or enslaved, the right to own or attain guns. All these years later, over a century after emancipation, Black people are still not guaranteed safety even through legal means of gun ownership. We are still killed for carrying guns that are acquired in accordance with law because blackness itself a threat and Black people are more likely to be extrajudicially killed for even being imagined to have a gun, whether permitted by law or not.

When the Black Panthers asserted in their Ten-Point Program their right to bear arms, they did so using the words of the U.S. Constitution. Point seven states: "We believe we can end police brutality in our Black community by organizing Black self-defense groups that are dedicated to defending our Black community from racist police oppression and brutality. The Second Amendment to the Constitution of the United States gives a right to bear arms. We therefore believe that all Black people should arm themselves for self-defense." In a critique of the New Black Panther Party, Lorenzo Kom'boa Ervin, a former Black Panther himself, denounces "romantic urban guerrillaism, which appeared at the period of the deterioration of the BPP in the mid-1970s." Ervin laments forms of vanguardism like small group terror and adventurism, saying they should be "avoided at all costs" because "too many militants were killed, arrested and exiled in the previous Panther formations to let a new movement think it can posture around with guns as a studio prop."[30]

Ervin's condemnation of irresponsible posturing leads us to better understand why contemporary self-defense politics must be meaningful. To the best of our ability, we should ensure our contemporary political formations are not just new iterations of the past. The Panthers were infiltrated and destroyed by government forces like the FBI's Counterintelligence Program (COINTELPRO), a covert operation that harmed and killed many throughout the Black community, among others. If our organizations are to provide societal and community value, we cannot aspire to form a mass movement of would-be martyrs that romanticize revolutionary armed struggle without having any weaponry, gun politics, or even skills with firearms.

Gun control is often a reaction to the threat posed by insurrectionary blackness. Hopes to stop the Black Panthers' efforts to organize armed community self-defense were the

30. Ervin, *Anarchism and the Black Revolution*, 134.

basis for the Mulford Act, a 1967 California firearms law criminalizing the open carrying of loaded firearms and passed in explicit response to their armed neighborhood patrols. The turbulent summer of 1967, when rebellions shook Detroit and Newark, led Congress to propose new gun restrictions after armed Black people resisted the police and National Guard who were attempting to implement martial law. It was no surprise when the Omnibus Crime Control and Safe Streets Act of 1968 was passed, considering these events and the assassinations of President John F. Kennedy, his brother Robert F. Kennedy, and Martin Luther King Jr. throughout the sixties (the latter two killed in the same year as the act's passage). It is arguable that each of those assassinations occurred as a result of public perceptions about each respective targeted person's relationship to Black struggles of the 1960s. The Kennedy brothers were and still often are seen as symbols of white liberal sympathy to Black civil rights, and King, of course, was a prominent movement leader. Their deaths would ultimately become part of the reasoning used in regulating firearms in a way that did not improve the lives of Black people or even make us safer. Despite the repeatedly demonstrated threat posed by armed white men, the fear of Black people and Black armed insurrection was a primary driver of gun control, not the desire to protect. Contemporary discourses about gun control cannot ignore the inherently racialized and reactionary nature of the state's attempts to regulate arms.

Guns are dangerous commodities that wreak havoc around the globe every day. They bring chaos and harm to many of our neighborhoods and communities. Although we invoke historical narratives of armed Black self-defense, we cannot ignore the almost inextricable links between gun violence and domestic and intimate partner violence, most notably against women. The weapons, however, are tools, just like many of the other commodities that drive oppression and destabilization around the world, and the conversation around gun control cannot simply be limited to partisan binaries supporting or opposing the ability to access firearms. Rather, these conversations should be grounded in far wider social discussions of hegemonic masculinity, the violent nature of white political expression, centuries of anti-Black racial violence, the delegitimization of Black community self-defense against state violence, the definition of "violence" itself, the undue political influence of the National Rifle Association and the gun lobby, violence against women, and so on. The debate on whether we choose to use guns as tools for our self-defense is reasonable to have in our community, but our adversaries have already expressed lack of interest in such a dialogue or debate. While the risk of trying to engage enemies in civility is indeed a necessary part of any movement, so too is a willingness to fight if and when necessary.

To accept the false retellings of history regarding the U.S. project is to believe that genocide, enslavement, and innumerable racialized brutalities were missteps in a historical moral arc toward progress and justice. Patriotism is ultimately self-destructive for Black people; patriotism necessarily comes at the expense of Black people. To be committed to a national project without any commitment from the state to reciprocate our needs for human rights means to labor against centuries of Black struggle. When we acknowledge the blackness of resistance, we acknowledge that "what happens to blacks indicates the truth (rather than the totality) of the system," as Jared Sexton notes. "Every analysis that attempts to account for the vicissitudes of racial rule and the machinations of the racial state without centering Black existence within its framework—which does not mean simply listing it among a chain of equivalents—is doomed to miss what is essential about the situation."[31]

31. Jared Sexton, "Racial Profiling and the Societies of Control," in *Warfare in the American Homeland: Policing and Prison in a Penal Democracy*, ed. Joy James (Durham: Duke University Press, 2007), 212.

Our self-defense understanding must account for the history of resistance in this country that has been so largely Black-led while also making the most of our history as diverse people. No one need be ignored, dismissed, or overlooked for their contributions. No matter what community or region we are from, no what color our skin, the struggle of Black people in the United States can inspire without being commodified by other movements. Black resistance and meaningful self-defense organizing opportunities are all around us. But the organizing we need to counter white supremacist capitalism has to be sincere and serious in a world that overemphasizes symbolic victories. Our liberation will feature the most disenfranchised among us overcoming the burdens of oppression.

Gang members, incarcerated people, the formerly incarcerated, and those cast away by society must be included and defended in our communities. They have been swallowed up by the reductive good-versus-bad binary constructed by white supremacist demands for perfect victimhood. The state intends to portray all of those who oppose it as criminals, thugs, and gangsters; other labels too are used, often ones associated with blackness regardless of actual ethnicity. When we allow these definitions of disposability, we support the state's necropolitical agenda, which dictates that the murder of certain people is unjust while the murder of others is acceptable or normal. The state does not—rather, it should not—have the right to kill anyone, armed or unarmed, whether perceived to be "guilty" or "innocent," and reproducing state definitions of guilt and justice places all marginalized communities at risk. Blackness is clearly seen as inherently criminal and guilty. Such logic rationalizes the killing of Black people by police, vigilantes, and others in response to the imagined existential threat posed to whiteness.

Those who have been cast away by society, who are despised even among our respective oppressed peoples, understand conflict perhaps better than any of us. The outcasts must be politicized once again, just like many gangs, inmates, and subjected Black people were politicized at the root of their organizations during the Black Power and civil rights movements. Here, the OG's, generals, and established members must use their credibility to make the needed transformations. Meanwhile those becoming politicized should become so in a way that is respectful and reflective of their knowledge and experiences. In this way, our movement efforts could be much more inclusive.

Precautionary self-defense goes far beyond traditional models of preparation. We live in a world where warfare and conflict have moved on technological fronts. Self-defense also means defending our right to privacy online and offline, and information security (also known as InfoSec) must be a priority. The Black community has an especially intimate relationship to being surveilled, experimented on, and treated as foreigners inside "our own country."

When Black people resist repression, the state acts against any uprising (and even a peaceful politics of autonomy and self-sufficiency) like it would against a foreign enemy. Take, for example, the 1921 massacre in the Greenwood community (also known as Black Wall Street) of Tulsa, Oklahoma. There police worked in concert with white mobs, one illustration of state repression in the long history of the state's collaboration with white vigilantism. The Greenwood community was bombed with airplanes and shot at with machine guns (these technologies were fairly new at the time). The anarchistic and noncitizen nature of blackness positions us as foreign invaders and threats to white order.[32] Enslaveability—the foundation of perpetual Black subordination and the essence of white supremacist capitalism's intention for Black people—trans-

32. It was reported by the *Guardian* that troops deployed to Ferguson, Missouri, during the protests after the killing of Michael Brown "used highly militarized language such as 'enemy forces' and 'adversaries' to refer to citizen demonstrators." Joanna Walters, "Troops Referred to Ferguson Protestors as 'Enemy Forces,' Emails Show," *Guardian*, April 17, 2015.

forms our respective neighborhoods into war zones. In the age of drones and lethal robotics, future violence against Black people will be increasingly nonhuman. That is to say, all of the oppressive mechanisms we fight against are being shaped, installed, and programmed into the entrails of robots designed for police work. It is of the utmost importance that we understand that robots designed and programmed in a white supremacist society will carry the logics of white supremacy. We must be prepared to defend ourselves against the likes of any threat, human or nonhuman. Just like the dogs that have been sicced on Black people for quite some time, newly developed technologies will be used against us as "enemies of the state."

We do not need an army, leaders, or advanced weaponry to organize ourselves in our respective localities. We need self-determined people willing to work together in their communities. Ultimately, state oppression is not just a mechanical function, it's also an admission that united fronts among us are really a threat. We all wish that the issues we face could be resolved peaceably, but as George Jackson wrote: "Patience has its limits. Take it too far, & it's cowardice."[33] What are we still waiting for that we cannot be-

33. George Jackson, *Soledad Brother: The Prison Letters of George Jackson* (Chicago: Chicago Review Press, 1994), 61.

gin to define and seize for ourselves? Pseudo-optimistic hopes of reform feel numbing, and stagnation is no longer tolerable.

The work of building a sustained movement dedicated to defending ourselves is all about love. We have tolerated abuse for far too long, and now, if we must share a house with our abuser, we should be prepared to defend ourselves. There's no justification for the brutality we experience at the hands of white supremacist capitalism and all the forms of oppression that come with it. What we must come to understand is that a willingness to defend ourselves and our communities is rooted in politics of collective care. Rather than seeking vengeance and aiming to harm oppressors, our desire to defend ourselves should be rooted in our love for one another. We are not ready to fight because we love fighting. We are ready to fight because we are worth fighting for.

CHAPTER FOUR

FROM HERE ON OUT

In a capitalist society, capital is produced, circulated, accumulated, hoarded, and exchanged through a variety of complex mechanisms. These mechanisms are studied by intellectuals and critical theorists and often articulated in complicated ways that are difficult to grasp. Yet when it comes to the examination of social movements, the influence of money is often overlooked. The existence of corporate interests, philanthropic funders, and elite capital makes co-optation both alluring and almost inevitable. This dilemma facing any burgeoning Black protest movement affects the potential for sustained grassroots political work and movement-building. Over the past three decades, money and funding have become increasingly central to the Black-led movement against anti-Black state violence. In the eyes of liberal funders, sympathetic celebrities, and well-intentioned middle-class people, a donation is an easy way to support the cause. The energy of an uprising can

thus be diluted into a mere charity endeavor. Who ultimately stands to gain from this?

After Trayvon Martin was murdered and protests erupted around the country, many people looked for a way to lend support. Trayvon galvanized and became the face of a protest movement against racism and anti-Black violence that has dramatically altered U.S. political culture. Martin's image became a commodity—T-shirts, hoodies, and other items declaring "Justice for Trayvon" proliferated—and some even saw the purchase of products like Skittles or Arizona Iced Tea (which Trayvon was holding when he was on his way home prior to being murdered) as acts of solidarity. The makers of Skittles and Arizona Iced Tea stayed mum about this, playing it safe by simply issuing condolences to the Martin family. Solidarity was also expressed through countless hashtag declarations that others too were Trayvon, that they felt anger and sorrow in the face of racial terror and vigilante violence. But these expressions, especially from non-Black people, meant little. Anti-Black violence is so pervasive because there is an unequal distribution of vulnerability and victimization (even within the Black community).

Following this tragedy and countless other incidents of anti-Black violence, it became clear—if it wasn't already—

that T-shirt slogans and consumption-based politics were vastly insufficient responses. Relying too heavily on these forms of protest may make people feel like they've done something, but it directs energies away from the fight for transformative change. Even boycotts—such one against the city of Cleveland following the non-indictment of the police officers who killed Tamir Rice—are far from an effective response despite their historic usefulness at times. People's attention is drawn away as they respond to yet another incident of violence elsewhere.

For some time, financial interests have attempted to direct the priorities of Black protest movements and popular mobilizations. With foundation grants, however, come rules and constraints. Movements mutate into nonprofits, and activists become professionals, celebrities, and executive directors. Individuals come to represent causes that affect millions to the point that individuals' own visibility and profile rival and even eclipse the cause. Confrontational and power-contesting grassroots politics are contained, controlled, and redefined. This is the soft power of corporate capitalism and specifically of the nonprofit industrial complex, defined by Dylan Rodriguez as "the set of symbiotic relationships that link together political and financial technologies of state and owning-class proctorship and surveillance over public political intercourse, including and especially emergent progressive and leftist social movements, since about the mid-1970s."[1] Though posing as humanitarian or even relatively radical in nature, this complex is inextricably linked to the anti-Black carceral system and complements it. It is through the philanthropic championing of "the movement's more moderate and explicitly reformist elements" (for example, anticapitalist economic justice politics being watered down to ideas of Black capitalism sold as economic self-determination) that liberatory and revolutionary visions are destroyed.[2] Compromising and neutralizing political movements is inherent to the complex's very function.

The logic behind "if you can't beat them, join them" is specious. Instead it is evident that disruptive Black-led movements can be tamed with money from funders who don't truly have our best interests in mind as well as sup-

1. Dylan Rodriguez, "The Political Logic of the Non-Profit Industrial Complex," in *The Revolution Will Not Be Funded: Beyond the Non-Profit Industrial Complex*, ed. INCITE! Women, Gender Non-Conforming, and Trans People of Color Against Violence (Brooklyn: South End Press, 2007). Reprinted online at http://sfonline.barnard.edu/navigating-neoliberalism-in-the-academy-nonprofits-and-beyond/dylan-rodriguez-the-political-logic-of-the-non-profit-industrial-complex/.

2. Ibid.

port from political institutions. The nonprofit industrial complex and liberal power structures find and reward the writers, activists, and so-called leaders (selected on our behalf) who least threaten the status quo. When movements become tax-deductible and antiracist politics are reduced to a "Donate Here" button or a T-shirt, what is there for those wielding oppressive power to really be worried about?

Scholar and activist Keeanga-Yamahtta Taylor highlights the history of funding as a method for containing Black cultural and political movements before the civil rights movement. Taylor notes the ways elite funding sources frequently overdetermine the decision-making processes of Black progressive organizations. In her words: "Perhaps the largest issue with the foundations and funders is that these organizations also attempt to politically shape the direction of the organizations they fund.... Ultimately, funders and other philanthropic organizations help to narrow the scope of organizing to changing 'policy' and other measures within the existing system."[3] Foundation money disciplines movements in practices of "professionalization," which lead folks to emphasize and prioritize careerism and

3. Keeanga-Yamahtta Taylor, *From #BlackLivesMatter to Black Liberation* (Chicago: Haymarket Books, 2016), 179.

the expectation that political struggle should be externally funded.

Our movements and our work need to avoid neoliberal enticements to corporatize or commoditize or otherwise become caught in the gears of capitalist accommodationism. The problems faced by oppressed people in the United States are tragedies, not an economic and political opportunity for otherwise negligent parties and organizations. What we know about the nonprofit world and the liberal approach to activism is that it can completely detract from the sincerity of movements. Petitions, donate buttons, letters, hashtags, phone calls, and marches are surely ways to raise awareness and consciousness, but when these methods are used as the primary or even sole means of combating U.S. authoritarianism, we should begin to see them as more than just counterproductive. They can foster complacency and even serve as deterrents themselves, where mere awareness (or "awakening") is seen as a sociopolitical victory and end in itself. Liberal activism drives the creation and maintenance of what one could describe as *microwaveable movements*, political mobilizations created to respond to problems but not actually fix them. Rather than reject capitalism, they embrace it through the murky morality of "conscious consumerism," which lulls us into falsely believing that purchasing a product is a systems-shifting action. Though it may make us feel better to purchase products from a company that has publicly declared that Black lives matter or donates a part of their proceeds to community organizations, it changes nothing. Likewise reliance on corporate and foundational support only nurtures political dependency and does not push Black people toward liberation and self-sufficiency. (Google's nonprofit arm has donated over $32 million to racial justice organizations since 2015, but the company has notably participated in the displacement of Black communities through gentrification.)

This is not to suggest that donors have never played a positive role in movement-building or that economic hardship is desirable for organizers. People have been increasingly using online platforms to collectivize resources or crowdfund disaster relief efforts, bail funds, and other forms of support for victims of violence or people experiencing financial hardship. But, fundamentally, how does a movement protect itself from co-option by individuals and institutions eternally endowed with the structural capacity and mandate to divert political energy and direction? This question must frame much of our future work and be centered in Black movement debates. We must ask ourselves if the chapter in our history in which we were bought and sold by capitalism is one we want to continue writing and living. The questions of what needs to be accomplished and how to move forward are complex. Creating priorities for people who come from a range of diverse backgrounds but share commonalities based on only certain parts of our identities (sometimes reducible only to skin color) is incredibly difficult. Territorial and sectarian bickering actively hinders our pathways to freedom. We want liberation, but finding what liberation truly entails means thoroughly interrogating the past, understanding how that past has enabled this present, and then imagining and beginning to actualize a future in meaningful material ways. That future must be increasingly absent of the things threatening us most in this present. Envisioning Black liberation is necessarily the act of creating a new world. As Black as resistance is and has been, there is far too much revolutionary history to be watered down.

The United States is in for a rude awakening. A system whose contours were created and shaped through terrible brutalities can only be denounced and rejected. We must overcome the system that is in place, not only for ourselves but also for the sake of the entire world, whose fate, through the globalization of capitalism, is inextricably entangled with that of the United States. The nationalism-rooted logic that drives so much of today's activism is counterproductive in our movements. We cannot have notions of liberation predicated on positively reclaiming the "real" American values that supposedly include "liberty and justice for all," and we cannot allow the state to misleadingly manipulate and exploit potentially liberatory endeavors. The country that we truly love or want to love does not exist yet, and what Black people generally articulate as a love of "our" country is not a love of the state. The rights that we cherish have come as a result of militant liberation work. They are a product of Black resistance and Indigenous rebellion, of colored defiance. It will surely continue to be this way because our survival has always hinged upon our people's willingness to counter the onslaught against us.

What we believe and who we are is so much more than the identities imposed upon us, first by European empires and then within the U.S. nation-state. Our self-determination does not depend on the stability and continued existence of what we have been deluded into believing is a "free country." Black liberation must mean the end of the United States as we understand it because this country's existence is dependent on the production of anti-blackness

to function as it does. The central question about Black liberation is not whether our claims to freedom are legitimate. As Lorenzo Kom'boa Ervin says, we "have the moral and political right to rebel."[4] The questions are when and how this collective effort will happen.

We must remember that material change-making need not necessarily be dramatic, and the expectation of change as solely sudden and cataclysmic is unreasonable. Building a new and innovative Left should be a primary concern, but it is important to remain free from the constraints of Left sectarian dogma, cults of personality, and selfish jostling to be recognized as "movement leaders." We can organize humbly and horizontally and resist the stratification of more easily destructible movements past, and we do not need leaders in any classical sense. While infighting and schisms that plagued movements of the past provide useful examples to avoid, past successes also need to be examined without romanticizing them. If our only purpose is to mimic the revolutionaries of previous generations rather than to improve upon their theory and methods, then we risk repeating their errors and reproducing their

4. Lorenzo Kom'boa Ervin, "Black People Have a Right to Rebel," *Libcom.org*, July 29, 2005, https://libcom.org/library/black-people-right-rebel-ervin.

harms. Some may argue that the need for a more singular and centralized movement is rooted. But we have seen how mass movements have been splintered and destroyed by the state's targeting and elimination of movement leaders. We have also seen (and continue to see) the elitism, community disconnect, and pandering to systems of power that come with individuals positioning and communicating themselves as movement leaders. Given the almost innate corruptibility of movement leadership in these ways, it is worth earnestly interrogating whether we need these conventional structures at all and, if so, how we could benefit from more horizontal and autonomous organizing.

Commentary about the anarchistic nature of blackness is not necessarily advocacy for anarchist politics or ideology. Rather it describes a condition that might lend itself to a form of organization reflecting that tendency. Blackness itself is anarchistic as a result of Black exclusion from the social contract (and thus non-assimilation into the state). This existence and a reflexive understanding of our existence within a color-based caste system can predispose us to be more readily primed for radical politics, which include anarchist and anti-authoritarian ideas. Why not directly challenge the authority of oppressive political institutions when our social placement primes us to do so?

"Anarchism" is a misnomer, really, to describe a set of politics that challenges the necessity of systems and structures that we presume to be necessarily like the state itself, with hierarchical and authoritarian governance. "Anarchy" is not synonymous with "chaos," and chaos is not an inevitability in a society that's supposed to value egalitarianism and therefore should reject the imposition of stratified social organization. The idea of creating a liberatory society outside of the confines of the U.S. nation-state is so abstract that many people presume chaos. Even some Black Americans feel that our ancestors' precolonial existence—a non-state existence prior to the European drawing of borders—was some sort or chaos or anarchy or even a more primitive means of organization. We can attribute that much to Eurocentric revisionist history and our own internationalization of that white supremacist miseducation. Any chaos attributed to African nations was largely a result not of self-organization but of colonial plunder and exploitation.

It would serve well to examine the history of trying to instill in Black people a fear of radical politics. One need only to look to the history of the "outside agitator" as a tool for dissuading Black people from interracial coalitions and left politics. During the civil rights movement, white antisegregationists who organized voter registration drives in the South were described by conservative politicians as "agitators" for disrupting the relative peace of Jim Crow racism. In contemporary activism, the suggestion that Black Lives Matter or other Black-led racial justice organizations are engineered by George Soros is a dismissive antisemitic insinuation that Jewish people are puppeteers funding Black organizing as a part of a so-called global takeover.[5] The idea of "Jewish communists" sowing seeds of racial unrest was also a part of reactionary white discourse during the Freedom Rides of 1961, which suggested Jewish outsiders were somehow responsible for manipulating and coordinating the bus rides. If or when Black people are radicalized in mass, if uprisings turn into sustained resistance against the state, the results would be or will be transformative. This is not to impose a special responsibil-

5. The canard of a global Jewish conspiracy is rooted in *The Protocols of the Elders of Zion*, an antisemitic text created in tsarist Russia in 1903. It described an alleged meeting attended by Jewish leaders (the "Elders of Zion") conspiring to take over the world. The text has twenty-four different protocols about different methods of conquest, propaganda, and control of the press, and control of financial systems that mirror contemporary tropes about Jewish control of banks and the media. Adolf Hitler endorsed these protocols in the early 1920s, and they became a part of Nazi propaganda against Jewish communities in Germany and across Europe.

ity for Black people to actualize freedom for everyone else (as is the subtextual commentary in liberal declarations that "Black women will save us" given their consistent progressive or practical voting decisions). Instead it suggests that Black people's place in the fight against white supremacist capitalism is unique since so much of structural violence entails anti-blackness. Failing to recognize this undermines the potential and efficacy of any widespread interracial coalitions (e.g., historical groups like the Chicago-founded Rainbow Coalition, which included the Black Panther Party, the Young Lords, a Puerto Rican leftist group, and the Young Patriots, an organization of white working-class leftists).[6]

Blackness is the anti-state just as the state is anti-Black. The oppression of Black people ought not to inspire the modification of this existing state or the aspiration to create a purportedly better state. Somehow during the formation of the U.S. settler project, anti-Black violence became

6. Amy Sonnie and James Tracy's *Hillbilly Nationalists, Urban Race Rebels, and Black Power: Community Organizing in Radical Times* (Brooklyn: Melville House Publishing, 2011) traces the history of interracial coalitions throughout the 1960s and 1970s. Among the groups highlighted in this work are the aforementioned Rainbow Coalition, as well as Rising Up Angry, the October 4th Organization, White Lightning, JOIN Community Union, and others that organized around shared ideological positions and resource provision in impoverished urban and rural areas.

a nod to the supposed beauty of the empire. Since the death of Crispus Attucks, the first person killed in the Boston Massacre (and thus the first martyr of the American Revolution), Black sacrifice for the nation has been turned into a weapon against us for the benefit of the state. As opposed to recognizing Black Americans as a group of people upon whose suffering the state is constructed, we too often understand the acquisition of Black rights and the eventual inclusion (assimilation) of Black people into the social contract as a reason to continue our fight within state apparatuses. The myth of the arc of social progress flies in the face of the reality that our rights are being actively rolled back and continuously denied. Understanding the anarchistic condition of blackness and the *impossibility* of its assimilation into the U.S. social contract, however, could be empowering. It is not up to us to castigate anyone who is or isn't empowered by our particular set of worldviews. We do not label anyone's philosophy right or wrong unless it reproduces or perpetuates existing oppressions. We simply hope to observe and analyze and express our concerns, rooted in the desire to achieve liberation for all Black people around the world.

As the authors of this book, we represent different aspects of blackness in this country, one of us as a descendant of enslaved Africans and the other as a child of Zimbabwean immigrants. We came together in the hopes of fulfilling something much bigger than ourselves, to offer a framework for understanding the Black condition in the United States and to challenge an increasingly standardized reaction to oppression. This imperfect yet heartfelt undertaking was intimidating, given all that we know needs to be accomplished and how much we *don't* know about how to define completion, an arrival at the destination where we wish to go. It is possible that a people's liberation is a perpetual project and must consistently be renewed and updated. Embracing Nina Simone's definition of freedom as the absence of fear, we strive to overcome our own fears to offer our understanding of structural violence, ways of subverting these systems, and ways to imagine new ones.

For many people, the difficult and enduring questions about racial capitalism and white supremacy can be overwhelming. People may ask for answers as though there are distinct formulas for overcoming each form of systemic oppression. The truth is almost reductively simple. The solution to capitalism is anticapitalism. The solution to white supremacy is the active rejection of it and the dual affirmation of Indigenous sovereignty and Black humanity. We must reject the violent machinations of the settler state (e.g., mass incarceration, treaty violations, transmisogyny, and so on). Any solution to the centuries of injustices and brutality waged against us requires a long struggle, and a crucial part of that struggle is precision in identifying our position as oppressed people and the structures that produce and maintain anti-blackness. Political education that thoroughly indicts racial capitalism and its supporting systems slowly increases consensus around our oppression. With this the chances increase for effective diverse actions necessary for liberation.

Removing oppression, not reforming it, demands the creation and radicalization of new dissidents. It is an exercise in imagining new communities. Our identities will be reflected in our willingness to nurture and channel the angst, anger, dissatisfaction, and resentment felt by Black people toward institutions of injustice. Channeling collective racial trauma into world-imagining energy and analysis is one of the ways we express care for our fellow Black people and our desire to improve their conditions. Nonparticipation in the systems that harm us is not a choice for many of us, but we can learn to undermine them when opportunities present themselves. Meaningful steps toward liberation do not have to be dramatic. Steve Biko's assertion that "the most potent weapon of the oppressor is the mind of the oppressed" encourages us to create new ways of understanding oppression so that we may effectively challenge it and re-create ourselves at every opportunity.

The ability to thrive as people is something beautiful, and we cannot allow ourselves to be disposed by being misused in this stale U.S. project of empire. Instead, we should be radically defining what will bring about our freedom from our unacceptable conditions. Until then rebellion will continually bring us closer to where we should rightfully be. When the work of our struggle settles beyond the turbulent waves of our current predicament, what lies in our depths can grow as a foundation to create a world free of oppressive violence, fear, and perpetual disruption.

LIST OF ILLUSTRATIONS

INDEX

"Passim" (literally "scattered") indicates intermittent discussion of a topic over a cluster of pages.

AK Press is small, in terms of staff and resources, but we also manage to be one of the world's most productive anarchist publishing houses. We publish close to twenty books every year, and distribute thousands of other titles published by like-minded independent presses and projects from around the globe. We're entirely worker run and democratically managed. We operate without a corporate structure—no boss, no managers, no bullshit.

The Friends of AK program is a way you can directly contribute to the continued existence of AK Press, and ensure that we're able to keep publishing books like this one! Friends pay $25 a month directly into our publishing account ($30 for Canada, $35 for international), and receive a copy of every book AK Press publishes for the duration of their membership! Friends also receive a discount on anything they order from our website or buy at a table: 50 percent on AK titles, and 20 percent on everything else. We have a Friends of AK e-book program as well: $15 a month gets you an electronic copy of every book we publish for the duration of your membership. You can even sponsor a deeply discounted membership for someone in prison.

E-mail friendsofak@akpress.org for more info, or visit the Friends of AK Press website: akpress.org/friends.html.

There are always great book projects in the works—so sign up now to become a Friend of AK Press, and let the presses roll!